THE
RUGBY
LEAGUE
MISCELLANY

THE
RUGBY
LEAGUE
MISCELLANY

BY DAVID LAWRENSON

VSP

Vision Sports Publishing
2 Coombe Gardens,
London SW20 0QU

www.visionsp.co.uk

Published by Vision Sports Publishing. 2007

ISBN 10: 1-905326-30-0
ISBN 13: 978-1-905326-30-3

Printed and bound in the UK by
Cromwell Press Ltd, Trowbridge, Wiltshire

Typeset by Palimpsest Book Production Limited,
Grangemouth, Stirlingshire

A CIP catalogue record for this book is
available from the British Library

Foreword
By Martin Offiah

I'm delighted to write the foreword of this book, which is packed full of facts, stats, records and stories from the rich history of rugby league. I think I broke my first try-scoring record at the age of 11 at Woolverstone Hall School when we played a rugby-type game called Stonehenge . . . and it just went on from there.

I never got sick of it. When the new Wembley opened in 2007 I was invited along to open a bar commemorating the try I scored in the 1994 final. I met Eddie Waring's son and it reminded me of just how far I'd come from being a kid sitting in Hackney, north London, watching rugby league on television. From the age of 21 my life has been about rugby league, and I owe the sport a great debt.

My introduction to the sport was watching the Challenge Cup final on television every year, and the first one I remember seriously sitting down and watching was the Halifax v St Helens match in 1987. It was a great game and that opened my eyes to rugby league. I was slightly in awe because the game seemed so tough and I could never imagine myself playing it. But I was also aware that Terry Holmes, the Welsh rugby union scrum half, had signed for Bradford Northern for quite a lot of money. That made me prick my ears up and I thought "maybe one day".

I thought perhaps that, when I'd played for England and done all the things I wanted to do in union, rugby league might be an option further down the line. But then I played for the Barbarians and in the Hong Kong Sevens and Middlesex Sevens, which were all on television. Doug Laughton, the Widnes coach, happened to be watching and was in need of a winger. I'd played cricket for Essex seconds during the summer alongside Nasser Hussain, so when Doug made an offer the idea of being a professional sportsman appealed to me.

The pages of this book are packed with rugby league facts, figures, stories and records, and I am lucky enough to feature in some of them. The first record I broke in rugby league came in my first season with Widnes. I hadn't scored in the opening two matches but in the third I did and went on to score in 15 straight games. I always loved scoring tries, the happiest time was the moment just before and just after scoring when you'd experience great emotion.

Having said that, scoring tries did become something of a burden during my career; I've lived and died by my try-scoring record. It got to the stage at Widnes where it was more newsworthy if I didn't score than if I did. Even off the field I managed to break the transfer record when I moved from Widnes to Wigan. That put pressure on me because when I didn't score people would be chanting "what a waste of money".

Of all the tries I scored, the one for Wigan against Leeds in the 1994 Challenge Cup final is the one that people often talk about and I can remember it vividly. When I put the ball down over the line I felt the hairs stand up on the back of my neck, it was the most euphoric feeling. To do it on such a big stage as well, it's what people dream about. The only way I can describe that feeling is that it must be what people feel when their six numbers come up on the Lottery. It's like someone giving you the best gift ever. There were so many emotions all rolled into one it was mind blowing.

Two years earlier I'd scored a record 10 tries for Wigan against Leeds in a Premiership semi-final at Central Park. When I tell people about that I look at their faces and it's as though it's not real. Sometimes I don't believe it myself. I always knew I would score a silly amount of tries in a game one day and that was the day that I did. In the early days of my career people thought I couldn't even play the game but records speak for themselves.

I hope you enjoy this cracking little book. It's a great read.

Martin Offiah

Acknowledgements

I would like to thank Ray Fletcher, the Rugby Football League's statistician, who not only contributed to this book but was a great point of reference whenever I needed confirmation or enlightenment on a particular topic. Thanks also to Charles Nevin of *The Independent*, a huge rugby league fan who provided me with a number of wonderful anecdotes about the game.

I am also indebted to Jim Drewett and Toby Trotman of Vision Sports Publishing for allowing me to indulge my passion for all things weird and wonderful about rugby league. Jim was a particularly supportive and encouraging editor and a joy to work with.

As with all books of this type, while I have endeavoured to check and double check everything the odd omission and inaccuracy will occur. Please try not to let it drive you mad and I would be extremely appreciative if you could contact me through the publishers if you either happen to discover an error or omission, or if you know of any story that might be of interest for future editions of the book.

David Lawrenson

— THE ORIGINS OF RUGBY LEAGUE —

The roots of rugby league can be traced back to a meeting at the George Hotel in Huddersfield in 1895. It was here that a group of northern clubs decided to break away from the Rugby Football Union and form the Northern Rugby Football Union.

The cause of the breakaway was the RFU's refusal to allow any kind of payment to players, although it was as much about powerful clubs wanting more of a say in how the game was run. Rugby had become a popular sport throughout Britain in the 19th century, although in Lancashire and Yorkshire it had taken particular hold in the booming towns and cities following the industrial revolution.

Unlike the professional classes, men who worked in the factories and mills had to take time off work if they wanted to play rugby and as such would be out of pocket. These working men represented the bulk of the northern clubs who wanted to make up the lost wages of their players which became known as "broken time" payments. However, the London-based RFU saw this as the first step on the slippery slope to professionalism. They believed in the amateur ethos and so they opposed it.

Clubs from the north were beginning to dominate the sport and the introduction of county competitions had fuelled their success. The RFU became concerned at the transfer of players between clubs and suspected inducements were being offered so they set up stringent rules and ruthlessly enforced them.

By the 1890s the Northern clubs had had enough and, having had their proposal for broken time payments rejected by a meeting of the RFU, in 1893 decided to go it alone. Twenty-one clubs met at the George Hotel on 29th August: Batley, Bradford, Brighouse Rangers, Broughton Rangers, Dewsbury, Halifax, Huddersfield, Hull, Hunslet, Leeds, Leigh, Liversedge, Manningham, Oldham, Rochdale Hornets, St Helens, Tyldesley, Wakefield Trinity, Warrington, Widnes and Wigan.

All but Dewsbury, whose committee hadn't had time to mandate their representative, resigned from the Rugby Football Union and the Northern Rugby Football Union was born. Two other clubs, Stockport and Runcorn, subsequently joined and the first fixtures in the new competition took place on 7th September.

Although the Northern Union intended to remain amateur and adhere strictly to broken time payments only, within three years they had agreed to legalise professionalism, although the players still had to have bona fide jobs. They soon realised that in order to continue to attract the crowds, they needed to make the game more spectator-friendly.

Gradually the points system was changed, line-outs were abolished, rucks and mauls were replaced by a play-the-ball system and they dispensed with flankers, bringing the number of players down from 15 to 13. In 1922, the Northern Union was renamed the Rugby Football League.

— WILLIAM WEBB WHO? —

Legend has it that a pupil of Rugby School, William Webb Ellis, invented the modern game of rugby in 1823 when, as a 16-year-old, he took the ball in his arms and ran with it. This story has been enshrined in rugby union folklore and a plaque at his old school states that William "with a fine disregard for the rules of football as played in his time, first took the ball in his arms and ran with it, thus originating the distinctive feature of the Rugby game."

All of which begs the obvious question, if the rules forbade running forward with the ball in hand, why wasn't he penalised?

Most games we know today originated in the public schools in the 18th and 19th centuries. Each school played football to its own particular set of rules but it seems that the version popular at Rugby was particularly appealing and when pupils went on to university and then out into the world they took their form of football with them and it prospered.

In his excellent book, *Rugby's Great Split – Class, Culture and the Origins of Rugby League Football*, Tony Collins argues that the propagation of the Ellis story was just a handy bit of PR exploited by the rugby union authorities at a time when the game was in turmoil. He writes, "Ellis's name was first advanced in 1877, and again in 1880, by Matthew Bloxham, an old boy keen to prove that the Rugby game was unique to itself and was not a variant of old folk football. Other than Bloxham's writings, Ellis's name is not mentioned in connection with the Rugby game in any work on the subject published before 1895. Even the 1895 inquiry of the Old Rugbeian Society into the origins of the game, which endorsed Bloxham's theory and led to the erection of the commemorative plaque, could not find a single witness who either saw Ellis's act or could provide hearsay evidence of it."

It didn't stop the rugby union authorities from naming their World Cup, the William Webb Ellis Trophy. Ellis, who was apparently born in Salford, died in Menton in the south of France in 1872 and is buried there.

— ERIC'S UNCLE JACK —

Jack Bartholomew, a stand off for Huddersfield who went on the first Great Britain (Northern Union) tour of Australia and New Zealand in 1910, was the uncle of comedian Eric Morecambe (real name John Eric Bartholomew). He broke two ribs in a warm-up match and didn't feature in the Test team. Apparently he only gained selection because Tommy Barton of St Helens withdrew at the last minute after the Northern Union had refused to make up his wages to his widowed mother while he was away, the extra £1 being given to dependent wives only!

— SUPER LEAGUE —

A century after the birth of rugby league the game went through another upheaval with the formation of Super League and a move to summer rugby. On 8th April 1995 the Rugby Football League's chief executive Maurice Lindsay revealed that News Ltd, owners of satellite broadcaster BSkyB, were prepared to pay £87m over five years for a Super League of 14 clubs playing in summer.

However, this would involve some clubs merging and the establishment of two new clubs in France. Those outside this elite competition would play in the First Division and would each be given a one off payment of £100,000.

The clubs in the new Super League would be Bradford Northern, Calder (Castleford, Featherstone Rovers and Wakefield), Cheshire (Warrington and Widnes), Cumbria (Barrow, Carlisle, Whitehaven and Workington Town), Halifax, Humberside (Hull and Hull Kingston Rovers), Leeds, London, Manchester (Oldham and Salford), Paris, South Yorkshire (Sheffield and Doncaster), St Helens, Toulouse and Wigan.

There were massive protests over the merger plans and even a debate in the House of Commons. When the dust settled the new competition kicked off with 12 clubs: Bradford Northern, Castleford, Halifax, Leeds, London Broncos, Oldham, Paris, St Helens, Sheffield, Warrington, Wigan and Workington Town. The first match took place at the Charlety Stadium in Paris on 29th March 1996 when Paris St Germain beat the Sheffield Eagles 30–24.

— BRADFORD'S CONVERSION —

Bradford City soccer club was a founder member of the Northern Union. They were called Manningham then and won the first championship, but left the union at the end of the 1903 season, changed their name, and joined Division Two of the Football League without ever having played a game of soccer.

— RUGBY LEAGUE AT THE OSCARS —

- "The British are coming," exclaimed Colin Welland in 1981 after winning an Oscar for his screenplay for *Chariots of Fire*. A huge rugby league fan, Welland was brought up in Newton-Le-Willows on the borders of St Helens and Warrington. He became an avid Warrington fan and is still seen at major games.

- Russell Crowe, who won an Oscar for his performance in *Gladiator* and has been nominated several times, is a massive rugby league fan. Although born in New Zealand he spent much of his early childhood in Australia and became a big fan of the South Sydney Rabbitohs.

  Even after finding fame in Hollywood Crowe remained a keen supporter, appearing at many home games, and supporting the club when they were out of the National Rugby League competition for two years. Crowe paid $40,000 for a brass bell used to open the first rugby league competition match in Australia in 1908, which he then returned to the club. In 2005, they became the first team in Australia to be sponsored by a film, when he negotiated a deal to advertise his movie *Cinderella Man* on their jerseys.

  In 2006 the members voted to allow Crowe and businessman Peter Holmes à Court to purchase 75 per cent of the club. He is friends with many current and former players of the club, and employed former South Sydney forward Mark Carroll as a bodyguard and personal trainer.

- Richard Harris and his co-star Rachel Roberts were both nominated for Oscars for their performances in the 1963 film *This Sporting Life* which centres on the life of rugby league player Frank Machin. Glenda Jackson, who had an unaccredited role in the film, later went on to win two Oscars for *Women in Love* in 1970 and A *Touch of Class* in 1973.

- Peter O'Toole, Oscar nominated eight times, was brought up in the Hunslet area of Leeds and is believed to have played rugby league in his youth.
- Diana Ross, who was part of the pre-match entertainment when England took on Australia at Wembley in the opening game of the 1995 World Cup, was nominated for an Oscar for her performance in the 1972 film *Lady Sings the Blues*.

— FATHERS AND SONS —

Ryan Giggs, the Manchester United and Wales footballer, is the son of Welsh rugby league player Danny Wilson who played for Swinton and once scored a record five drop goals in a game for the club. When his parents split up Ryan reverted to his mother's name of Giggs.

Another Manchester United legend, Bill Foulkes, who won just about every honour, including a European Cup winner's medal in 1968 during his 20 seasons with the club, was the grandson of Tom Foulkes who played for and captained St Helens and was an England international.

Playing at centre for Wigan in the first ever Wembley Challenge Cup final in 1929 was a Scot, Roy Kinnear, father of the famous comic actor also called Roy. Roy senior, who scored a try in Wigan's 13–2 cup triumph over Dewsbury, was also capped by Great Britain. He collapsed and died playing in a rugby union game for the RAF during the Second World War. His son died after falling off a horse filming *The Return of the Three Musketeers* in 1988.

Emlyn Hughes, the late Liverpool and England footballer, was the son of a Welsh rugby player, Fred, who played league for Barrow and Great Britain.

— RUGBY LEAGUE LEGENDS: MARTIN OFFIAH —

Chariots Offiah!

Martin Offiah was that rarest of rugby league legends, a player born and raised in London. Offiah is the greatest English try scorer in the history of the game and third in the all-time list behind Australian Brian Bevan and Welshman Billy Boston.

Offiah's exploits, lightning pace allied to a natural try-scoring instinct and a flair for showmanship, meant he transcended the boundaries normally associated with rugby league. Even years after he retired, if anyone outside the rugby league heartlands was asked to identify a rugby league player, Offiah's name was invariably the one that they came up with.

Born to Nigerian parents in Hackney, north London he went to Woolverstone Hall boarding school near Ipswich like his elder brother and soon earned a reputation as a good sportsman on the rugby pitch and the cricket field. However, he wasn't considered fast enough to get into the school's relay team and when he first dipped his toe into the world of professional sport, it was as a cricketer playing for Essex 2nd XI at the same time as Nasser Hussein.

On leaving school he joined Rosslyn Park rugby union club and began to make his mark by scoring some spectacular tries. He earned wider recognition when picked to play for the Penguins, a guest side, in the Hong Kong sevens and later in the Middlesex Sevens where his duel with Harlequins flyer and future England wing Andrew Harriman was the highlight of the tournament.

He was then chosen to play for the Barbarians on their Easter tour of south Wales. Doug Laughton, coach at Widnes rugby league club, saw Offiah on television, liked what he saw and made contact with him. Laughton convinced the 20-year-old that he had a big future in rugby league and signed him in the summer of 1987 without ever having seen him play in the flesh.

Offiah's move hardly merited a mention in the national press but in his first season in rugby league he proved a sensation, breaking the club's try-scoring record with 42 and helping them to win the championship. He went on to score 181 tries in 145 games for Widnes before joining Wigan in January 1991 for a fee of £440,000. This figure remained a record for a total cash transfer until 2006.

He played in Wigan's World Club Challenge win over the Brisbane Broncos in 1994, and notched up four Challenge Cup wins, five Championships, three Regal Trophy wins and one Lancashire Cup victory.

Offiah made a total of 158 appearances for Wigan with another single appearance as a substitute. He averaged more than a try a game, crossing the line 186 times. Within this total is the record ten tries he scored in a single match against Leeds in 1992. Against Leeds in the Challenge Cup Final in 1994 he scored what is widely acknowledged as the greatest try ever scored at the old Wembley Stadium. Collecting the ball under his own posts he rounded a number of tacklers before breaking out into open space. Only the Leeds full back Allan Tait, who had been a team-mate at Widnes, stood between him and the try line, but even Tait's first-hand knowledge of what Offiah could do failed to stop him touching down after which Offiah sank to his knees. In the new Wembley stadium this try is commemorated at the '1994 Bar'.

Soon after the introduction of Super League in 1996, Offiah entered into a unique deal to play rugby league for the London Broncos and rugby union for Bedford. In 1997 he was awarded the MBE and after picking it up at the palace he was whisked by helicopter to play for the Broncos at Warrington that evening and the following day crossed the Pennines to play for Bedford at Rotherham. He played in the last Challenge Cup final at the old Wembley, scoring a classic try in a defeat to Leeds. His final move took him to the Salford City Reds.

After retiring Offiah dabbled in acting and popped up on television in a variety of shows including the first series of the BBC's *Strictly Come Dancing*, coming fourth with his partner Erin Boag. In 2005 alongside Natasha Kaplinsky, he hosted the one-off special, *Strictly African Dancing*.

Martin Offiah
Born: 29th December 1966, Hackney
Position: Wing
Playing career: 1987–2004
Clubs: Widnes, Wigan, London Broncos, Salford City Reds, Easts (Aus), St George (Aus)
International record: Great Britain (33 apps, 26 tries), England (5 apps, 8 tries)
Scoring: 481 tries, 1 goal, 6 drop goals

— RELIGIOUS CONVERSION —

The only clergyman to play rugby league at the highest level was Australian Father John Cootes. A Roman Catholic priest from Newcastle, New South Wales, Cootes was ordained by the Pope and played rugby union while studying in Rome.

A centre, he made his international debut against New Zealand in 1969 and faced Great Britain when they toured Australia the following year. He was in the squad for the World Cup, which was held in Britain in 1970, and apparently used to start the day by saying mass at St Mary's church in Bradford.

Cootes was the top try scorer in the competition with five tries, including one against Great Britain in a bruising final at Headingley. He also touched down when Australia beat France in Perpignan on the way home.

Cootes later left the priesthood and after a spell as a television sports reporter set up a furniture business, John Cootes' Furniture Warehouse, which he still runs.

— HOW'S THAT —

Australian cricketer Ray Lindwall, who along with Keith Miller formed one of the best fast bowling partnerships in Test history, was also an impressive rugby league player. He played 31 first-grade games for St George from 1940 to 1946, scoring seven tries and kicking 123 goals for a total of 267 points before concentrating on cricket.

Lindwall played 61 cricket Tests between 1946 and 1959, taking 228 wickets at an average of 23.03 runs, and scoring 1,502 runs, which included three centuries as a late-order batsman with an average of 21.15.

He was described by Wisden as, "perhaps the man who established fast-bowling's role in the modern game".

— LONG DISTANCE GOALS —

Wigan's Joe Lydon is credited with landing the longest and possibly most famous drop goal in rugby league history, while playing in the 1989 Challenge cup semi-final against Warrington at Maine Road.

In a tense, closely fought contest, the scores were tied at 6–6 with seven minutes of the match remaining. Lydon got the ball just inside his own half and swung his boot to send it soaring through the posts. It was officially measured at 61 yards (just under 56 metres) and put his side 7–6 ahead. They eventually went on to win 13–6 and beat St Helens 27–0 in the final. "I just shut my eyes and hit it," said Lydon, "and every year that goes by, it gets a few yards longer."

Castleford's Arthur Atkinson landed the longest ever goal kick in a league match at St Helens on 26th October 1929. With the help of a strong wind he kicked a penalty from an amazing 75 yards (68.5 metres), which helped his side to a 20–10 victory.

The greatest goal kick ever seen at Wembley was Len Killeen's long distance effort for St Helens against Wigan in the 1966 Challenge Cup final. The South African wing had already landed one penalty, but the near 100,000 crowd gazed in disbelief as ten minutes into the game he lined up another from five yards inside his own half and ten yards from the touchline.

That too was successful and the Saints went on to win 21–2. Alex Murphy, the St Helens skipper, said later: "No-one expected him even to attempt a kick at goal, never mind grab two points."

— JIMMY YOUNG —

The singer turned DJ was born Leslie Ronald Young in Cinderford, Gloucestershire in the early 1920s. The son of a miner, he was an excellent boxer and rugby player and once turned down an offer of a professional career with Wigan rugby league club.

— NICKNAMES —

Rugby league has not been blessed with too many nicknames, but there are a few notable exceptions. One of the most famous was 'The Toowoomba Ghost', which was just perfect for Eric Harris. From the Australian town of Toowoomba, Harris became a record try scorer at Leeds, where his terrific speed enabled the winger to ghost past opponents down the touchline.

Vince Karalius was equally well known as 'The Wild Bull of the Pampas'. The original 'Wild Bull' was the Argentinian heavyweight boxer, Louis Firpo, who knocked the great Jack Dempsey out of the ring in an epic, brawling title fight. Karalius had the same crash, bang style that made him one of Great Britain's most feared forwards.

'Bomber' Harris was something of a derogatory title for Sir Arthur Harris, who as commander-in-chief of Bomber Command was one of the most controversial figures of the Second World War. However 'Bomber' was a term of great respect for the Hull and Great Britain hooker Tommy Harris who earned the nickname for his explosive running bursts.

Roger Millward was 'Roger the Dodger'. At 5ft 4in, Millward was one of the shortest players to gain Test honours and his dodging style made him extremely difficult to hold.

The 'Gentleman' prefix has been added to a few players, but perhaps the most famous and deserved was Gentleman Johnny Whiteley, the Hull Test forward who was never sent off in a long, illustrious career.

The 'Prince of Centres' was Harold Wagstaff, captain of Huddersfield and Great Britain over 80 years ago. The title says it all.

'Chariots' was an obvious epithet given to flying wing Martin Offiah, despite the fact that the proper pronunciation of his surname is 'Off-yer'. Steve 'Knocker'

Norton was a hugely talented loose forward for Castleford, Hull and Great Britain in the 1970s and early 1980s while Peter 'Flash' Flanagan was an outstanding hooker in the 1960s and 1970s for Hull, Hull Kingston Rovers and Great Britain.

— TOP 10 SUPER LEAGUE CAREER TRIES —

Tries	Player	Years
149	Keith Senior (Leeds, Sheffield)	1996–2006
127	Kris Radlinski (Wigan)	1996–2006
120	Robbie Paul (Huddersfield, Bradford)	1996–2006
111	Francis Cummins (Leeds)	1996–2005
108	Toa Kohe-Love (Warrington, Bradford, Hull)	1996–2006
108	Lesley Vainikolo (Bradford)	2002–2006
107	Keiron Cunningham (St Helens)	1996–2006
100	Paul Newlove (Castleford, St. Helens)	1996–2004
103	Sean Long (St Helens, Wigan)	1996–2006
97	Anthony Sullivan (St Helens)	1996–2001

Note: Stats correct up to and including season 2006.

— NOTHING TO BEAT —

An easy win is often summed up by saying the victors had 'nothing to beat'. But this was literally true of Huddersfield's defeat of Castleford in a 1941 Yorkshire Cup second round tie. At full-time it was 3–3 and extra-time was ordered. But this was wartime and several of the Castleford players had to report for duty. When they failed to return to the field, Huddersfield kicked off against no opposition, scored a try and kicked the goal. The referee then ended the game, which was later ratified as an 8–3 victory.

— TRIES IN A SEASON —

Huddersfield signed Albert Rosenfeld after Australia's inaugural 1908/09 tour of Britain and he went on to become one of the greatest ever imports. Yet he was not in the Kangaroos' squad when it was first selected. It was only after a massive public protest that he and two other players were drafted into the squad.

Tries	Scorer	Season
80	Albert Rosenfeld (Huddersfield)	1913–14
78	Albert Rosenfeld (Huddersfield)	1911–12
72	Brian Bevan (Warrington)	1952–53
71	Lionel Cooper (Huddersfield)	1951–52
68	Brian Bevan (Warrington)	1950–51
67	Brian Bevan (Warrington)	1953–54
66	Lionel Cooper (Huddersfield)	1954–55
63	Johnny Ring (Wigan)	1925–26
63	Eric Harris (Leeds)	1935–36
63	Jack McLean (Bradford Northern)	1951–52
63	Brian Bevan (Warrington)	1954–55
63	Ellery Hanley (Wigan)	1986–87

— GOLDEN POINT —

The 'Golden Point' is generally thought to be a modern idea to decide matches that finish even at the end of normal time. But the first time it was used was back in 1941, resulting in the longest ever match.

When Castleford met Featherstone Rovers in a wartime Challenge Cup first round tie it finished 3–3. After 20 minutes of extra-time the game was still locked at 5–5. It was then decided to continue until one side scored and the game finally ended when Castleford's Jim Croston scored a try in the 117th minute of play.

— TWELVE APOSTLES AND OTHERS —

Manchester Ship Canal once staged a Challenge Cup tie. It was not played in the canal, of course, but MSC was a non-League side who won through to the first round of the cup and lost 28–9 to Dewsbury in 1935.

Oddly named amateur clubs have long added a little extra colour to rugby league's most famous cup competition. There was Uno's Dabs, a team from a St Helens firm who made cloth wipes for machinery. They twice made it through to the first round in the 1930s.

United Glass Bottles were another St Helens outfit who were captained by the father of Ray French, the former Saints and Great Britain forward, when they lost 48–5 to Hunslet in 1939. The UGB factory was on the site of the proposed new St Helens ground.

The Twelve Apostles, meanwhile, were a Catholic church side in Leigh, who clearly gained no divine help as they were twice knocked out in the first round during the 1920s.

British Oil and Cake Mills regularly found the right cup ingredients and appeared in the first round six times between 1920 and 1971. Flimby and Fothergill, were not a firm of solicitors, but two adjoining Cumbrian villages, who suffered a St Valentine's Day massacre when they lost 116–0 to Wigan in 1925.

Half-Acre Trinity (1908), Purston White Horse (1910), Healey Street Adults (1920) and Triangle Valve (1956) were other junior clubs with bizarre names to have their day of Challenge Cup glory.

— RUGBY LEAGUE LEGENDS: ALEX MURPHY —

Alex Murphy: a true rugby great

One of the greatest rugby players of either code, Alex Murphy was born in St Helens on 22nd April 1939. He signed for his hometown club at the age of 16 and within three years had established himself as the best scrum half in the world.

During an eventful career he won every honour in the game and is the only player to captain three different sides to victory in the Challenge Cup final. As a coach he was no less successful, taking Leigh, Warrington, St Helens and Wigan to Wembley. Never afraid to speak his mind, he has courted controversy all his life and remains one of the game's larger than life characters.

Murphy was a schoolboy star at St Austin's school in the Thatto Heath area of St Helens. He was such a hot property that the St Helens officials had to employ cloak and dagger tactics to sign him just after midnight on his 16th birthday.

Most youngsters joining their local club would be happy to learn their trade for a few seasons at the lower levels – not Murphy. After just a couple of games in the 'A' team he wanted a first team spot and when he didn't get it demanded a transfer. Luckily, in coach Jim Sullivan, he found a mentor who was tough but inspirational. Murphy made his debut in the first team that season against Whitehaven, but afterwards Sullivan listed his mistakes and made him do extra training,

That additional training would include sprinting and his blistering acceleration allied to all his other gifts would make him a superstar. Murphy had everything, dazzling sidestep and swerve, lightning pace, a fine kicking game and a brilliant rugby brain. He was also cocky and had a touch of arrogance, which made him a formidable opponent.

He also proved himself in rugby union when doing his National Service in the RAF in the late 1950s. At that time, the armed forces were probably the only place where a rugby league player would be allowed to play union. His superiors certainly wanted such a talent in their team, although he did come into conflict with them at times.

On one occasion his commanding officer wanted him to play for the RAF but Murphy was adamant he was playing for St Helens. The officer threatened to post him to Guam if he didn't play for the RAF. Murphy had no idea where Guam was but when he found out it was a remote island in the Pacific Ocean, he quickly changed his mind.

In one match against Cambridge University he was pitted against the then England fly half, Richard Sharp. Murphy scored three tries in a dazzling display which moved Pat Marshall, the rugby union correspondent of *The Daily Express*, to describe him as, "One of the truly great players of our time."

In 1958 he became the youngest ever Great Britain tourist and on that tour to Australia Murphy's greatness was confirmed when he outplayed the Kangaroos' scrum half Keith Holman.

Meanwhile, St Helens were becoming a power in the game, reaching their peak in 1966 when they swept the board. However this was the beginning of the end of his time at Knowsley Road, the Saints had signed another great scrum half in Tommy Bishop and Murphy found himself at centre.

He was in dispute with the club and was eventually put on the transfer list. It seemed he would sign for Australian club North Sydney, but instead accepted a surprising offer to become player/coach at Leigh, his five-year deal making him the highest paid coach in the game. In 319 appearances for St Helens he had scored 175 tries and landed 42 goals.

Leigh were deeply unfashionable but his motivational presence led to one of the biggest upsets in Challenge Cup history when he led the side to cup final glory in 1971 against red hot favourites Leeds. As ever controversy was never far away. The Leeds skipper Syd Hynes became the first player to be sent off at Wembley after a clash with Murphy. Legend has it that the cocky scrum half winked while being taken off on a stretcher but Murphy himself disputes this. He returned to lead his side to glory.

Three years later he lifted the trophy again as player/
coach at Warrington after which he retired as a player. He
subsequently went on to coach Salford, Wigan, Leigh,
St Helens and Huddersfield. Murphy became a summariser
at BBC television for a spell, and was employed to write
opinion columns for newspapers such as the *Daily Mirror*
and the *Manchester Evening News*. One was known as
'Murphy's Mouth.'

An inaugural member of the rugby league Hall of Fame,
he was awarded the OBE in 1998.

Alexander James Murphy
Born: 22nd April 1939 St Helens, Lancashire
Position: Scrum half
Playing career: 1956–75
Clubs: St Helens, Leigh, Warrington
International record: Great Britain (27 apps, 16 tries)
Scoring: 275 tries, 184 goals

— DEBUT AT WEMBLEY —

Mike Smith's first senior match was at the great stadium.
The 22-year-old second row forward was a surprise
inclusion in Hull's team to meet Wakefield Trinity in the
1960 Challenge Cup final. With the Hull pack badly hit
by injuries, it was expected that reserve Colin Cole, who
had played in the Championship semi-final against
Wakefield a week earlier, would be retained. When he was
dropped, Cole immediately walked out and never played
for Hull again. Smith picked up a loser's medal and went
back to comparative obscurity, playing in only 20 more
matches for Hull.

— WHEN THE TOUGH GET GOING —

Rugby league players are known for their toughness – and rightly so because there have been many instances of players continuing to play with serious injuries.

In 1980 Roger Millward was captaining Hull Kingston Rovers in the Challenge Cup Final against bitter rivals Hull at Wembley. After 13 minutes Hull hooker Ron Wileman caught the little stand off high and late. Millward was pole-axed but managed to get up and despite suffering a broken jaw continued to the end of the game. Rovers won 10–5 and Millward even managed a bit of a smile when he received the cup from the Queen Mother.

He said later: "The bone was out of place and I could feel it wasn't right. Fortunately, a few seconds later, I went in to tackle Hull's Steve Norton and my jaw caught his knee. The impact caused my jaw to click back in place and I was able to carry on playing."

In the 1990 final, Wigan's Shaun Edwards suffered a double fracture of an eye socket and a depressed cheekbone in the tenth minute of the match against Warrington but refused to leave the field until a few minutes from the final whistle by which time Wigan had secured a 36–14 victory.

But the heroics of Great Britain skipper Alan Prescott top the lot. In 1958 the St Helens forward led Great Britain on a tour of Australasia. The tourists lost the first Test 25–8 in Sydney and in the second Test in Brisbane it looked like they were heading for another defeat. Prescott broke his arm just three minutes into the game and as there were no substitutes in those days, carried on. After 17 minutes, stand off Dave Bolton broke his collarbone and several other players received serious knocks.

Tour manager Tom Mitchell later described the scene in the dressing room at half-time: "I sat down beside the captain, his arm merely carried several folds of bandaging. The doctor in attendance at the game was summoned. His verdict was a positive one, 'This man cannot continue – and it must not be considered'.

"But when the team rose to go out Alan led them. If he hadn't done so the game was over – the quest for the Ashes blown away. He switched places with prop McTigue when he thought it was better to do so. He gathered the ball, he ran, he dictated the pattern of play and he tackled well with his good arm. Only those present at the game had any idea of the man's naked courage."

Prescott led his side to a memorable 25–18 victory and Great Britain went on to clinch the series.

— NEW GAME TAKES SHAPE —

Three major rule changes were made from the start of the 1906/07 season:

(1) Teams reduced from 15 to 13 players.
(2) Beginning of 'play-the-ball', introduced to prevent rucking and mauling. A tackled player was required to regain his feet before putting the ball down. Previously, a scrum followed after a player was tackled. Before that rule, a tackled player put the ball down in front of him without regaining his feet.
(3) A scrum would now be formed from where a player kicked the ball into touch without it bouncing – 'ball back'.

The rule changes meant the Northern Union game now became quite distinctive from that played by the Rugby Football Union. There was a dramatic rise in open play and scoring. The previous season Oldham had been top scorers with 446 points from 40 League matches. But in the first season of the radical rule changes nine clubs passed that points total and none played more than 34 matches.

— BOXING CLEVER —

Probably the only sport tougher than rugby league is boxing so it's not surprising that quite a few rugby league players have been useful boxers:

- **Anthony Mundine** was a hugely talented Australian stand off with the St George Dragons and the Brisbane Broncos in the 1990s but in 2000 he gave up rugby league for a career in boxing. His father, who had been a middleweight, trained him and after ten professional bouts Mundine fought for his first world title against IBF Super Middleweight champion Sven Ottke in January 2001. Ottke knocked him out in the tenth round but Mundine went on to claim the vacant WBA Super Middleweight title with a unanimous points decision over Antwun Echols on 3rd September 2003. He successfully defended his title once, before losing it on a split points decision against Manny Siaca. Mundine failed in his attempt to re-gain the WBA super middleweight title after losing to Mikkel Kessler on 6th August 2005.

- **Adam Fogerty** was a heavyweight boxer before hanging up his gloves to become a rugby league player. A talented prop, he joined the Halifax Blue Sox and later played for Super League champions St Helens before finishing his career with the Warrington Wolves.

   Fogarty then took up acting, playing a heavy in *Coronation Street* before landing big screen roles in *Shooting Fish*, the Guy Ritchie film *Snatch* and the film version of *Up 'n' Under*.

- **Solomon Haumono**, a tough forward born in Auckland of Tongan descent played in the NRL for the Manly-Warringah Sea Eagles, Canterbury Bulldogs, Balmain Tigers, St George Illawarra Dragons, and in Super League for Harlequins. Haumono, whose father Maile was a former Australian heavyweight champion, took time out of rugby after his spell with the St George Illawarra Dragons in 2000 to take up a career in professional boxing. He fought eight times between 2000 and 2002, winning all of his heavyweight contests inside the distance. Solomon was briefly the New South Wales heavyweight champion and rejected an offer to join the stable of American promoter Don King before returning to rugby league. Following a second spell with Manly in 2003, Haumono joined Harlequins and played in the capital for two seasons. In December 2006, with a year remaining on his contract, Haumono quit rugby league to return to professional boxing. He resumed his boxing career with a first round knockout on 7th March 2007.

- **Monty Betham** played for the New Zealand Warriors in the NRL before joining the Wakefield Trinity Wildcats in Super League. Betham represented New Zealand in eight Tests and also played for Samoa at the 2000 World Cup. In December 2006 he announced his retirement from rugby league in order to pursue a career in boxing. His first fight took place in Samoa on 31st March 2007 when he defeated Vai Toevai in six rounds. Betham's father, also called Monty, had 53 professional fights as a middleweight or light heavyweight from 1973–1982.

- **John Hopoate** turned to boxing after his controversial career in Australian rugby league with the Manly-Warringah Sea Eagles, Wests Tigers and the Northern Eagles ended following another lengthy suspension. On 17th May 2006 the Tongan won his debut fight after only 47 seconds of the opening round, knocking out Samoan Frank Faasolo. He won his next five fights but lost the following two.

— WORLD CUP: THE 1950s —

Rugby League was the first of the rugby codes to have a World Cup competition. It all began in 1954 and what followed has been eventful, colourful and sometimes downright bizarre.

As with the soccer World Cup and the modern Olympics we owe a debt of gratitude to a Frenchman. Paul Barriere was the young president of the French league who came up with the idea and got the support of Rugby Football League secretary Bill Fallowfield for a tournament in France.

The Australians weren't that keen but when the French Federation guaranteed to cover the travel costs and expenses of the teams they agreed to take part. The French donated the trophy, which was an impressive silver cup standing 30 inches high and weighing over half a hundredweight.

Just four nations took part in that inaugural event: Australia, New Zealand, Great Britain and France. It kicked off at Parc des Princes in Paris on 30th October 1954 with the host nation beating New Zealand 22–13.

The Australians, who had just beaten Britain in an Ashes series, were favourites to take the title, particularly as only three of the Great Britain tourists made themselves available. However, after all the teams had played each other, Britain and France topped the table on equal points leading to a play-off between the two European nations which became the first World Cup final. Scotsman Dave Valentine had the honour of lifting the trophy after Great Britain's 16–12 victory at the Parc des Princes.

The Australians staged the competition in 1957 and won it by topping the four-team table – there was no final play-off. It was Britain's turn to host the event three years later and they regained the trophy by heading the table, once again there would be no definitive final play-off. However, the crucial match, against the Australians, did nothing for the sport as it turned out to be a brutal contest in the mud at Odsal.

— 12-A-SIDE —

Rugby league would have been a 12-a-side game had the experiment of dropping three players been deemed a success in 1903.

In the early 1900s the game was still basically 15-a-side rugby union, but there were increasing demands to make it more open and exciting. One idea put forward was to reduce the number of players on the field and it was decided to try out 12-a-side rugby in representative matches during the 1903/04 season.

In fact, the very first international match was a 12-a-side affair with Other Nationalities beating England 9–3 at Wigan's Central Park on 5th April 1904. England actually began the game with only 11 players as James Lomas arrived after the kick-off. The teams lined up with four threequarters and five forwards, although earlier in the season the county championship formations were listed as three threequarters and six forwards.

Clubs were asked to give their opinions about the experiment and although a few were in favour, the new format was not put to the vote because it was unlikely to come anywhere near the 75 per cent majority needed to make the change.

— FASTEST TRY —

A try in seven seconds is the fastest reported touchdown in the game's history. It came straight from the kick-off and was scored by Oldham winger Chris Campbell at Doncaster in a National League One match on 18th May 2003. Oldham kicked off and when Doncaster's Paul Gleadhill fumbled the ball it went straight to Campbell who touched down. Nonetheless, the Doncaster Dragons recovered from this shock opening to win 52–24.

— RUGBY LEAGUE LEGENDS : HAROLD WAGSTAFF —

The Prince of Centres

Harold Wagstaff was the first superstar of the breakaway Northern Union. Known as the 'Prince of Centres', he was phenomenally gifted and earned his reputation as much for his skills as his fine rugby brain and leadership qualities.

Wagstaff was signed from the local Underbank amateur club for five gold sovereigns and it was the best money that

Huddersfield ever spent. A precocious talent, Wagstaff was only 15 when he played his first match for Huddersfield, which was against Bramley on 10th November 1906.

Huddersfield had assembled a formidable side, which was dubbed the 'Team of all Talents'. The forwards included the inspirational Duggie Clark and Ben Gronow, a goal kicking Welsh prop, who helped to provide possession for a phenomenal three-quarter line which included legendary try-scoring wing Albert Rosenfeld, Tommy Gleeson, Stanley Moorhouse and Wagstaff. They swept all before them, totally dominating the game in the early part of the 20th century. Arguably, Wagstaff was the most important player in the side. Big, strong and skilful his leadership skills were evident early on when he captained the club at 20.

In 1908 Wagstaff was selected for England against the first Australian tourists. He also featured in one of the greatest international matches of all time in 1914 which was dubbed the 'Rorke's Drift' Test after the heroic action by British soldiers in South Africa on which the film *Zulu* was based.

Wagstaff had been chosen to lead the second Northern Union side to tour Australia and New Zealand. Having agreed to play two Test matches in three days he baulked at the suggestion that they play the third Test five days later, not least because of the injuries which had devastated his squad following those two encounters. However, after a meeting of the Northern Union Council back in Britain he was ordered to play the match. They ended their instructions to the captain with the words borrowed from Nelson at the battle of Trafalgar, "England expects that every man will do his duty". They certainly did.

The match went ahead in Sydney and Wagstaff's injury-ravaged team found themselves down to ten players just before half-time. This was before the days of substitutes so they just had to soldier on. Leading 14–6, they managed to hang on until the final whistle thanks to a desperate rearguard action to record one of the most remarkable wins in Test Match history.

On his return Wagstaff led Huddersfield to an unprecedented sweep of all four cups in a season. Had it not been for the First World War he would have notched up more honours and earned many more international caps. Wagstaff played his last match against Oldham at Watersheddings in March 1925.

Harold Wagstaff
Born: 19th May 1891, Holmfirth, Yorkshire
Position: Centre
Playing Career: 1906–1925
Club: Huddersfield
International record: Great Britain (12 apps)
Scoring: 209 tries, 19 goals

— LONGEST SCORING RUN —

When David Watkins scored all of Salford's points with five goals in a 15–10 home defeat against Leeds in the opening match of the 1973/74 season, it was the start of a scoring run that would continue for a record 92 domestic matches. Watkins' run lasted from 19th August 1972 until 25th April 1974 and covered two whole seasons, which brought him 929 points from 41 tries and 403 goals.

The remarkable scoring sequence ended when he was injured on Great Britain's 1974 tour of Australasia and he missed the first eight of Salford's matches the next season.

Although Watkins made his name as a Wales rugby union fly half, he played in the centre throughout his scoring run apart from two matches on the wing.

— THEY SAID IT —

"Rugby league is war without the frills."
Anon

"If working men can't afford to play, they shouldn't play at all."
Harry Garnett, a leading figure in Yorkshire rugby union, at the time of the great split

"In south west Lancashire, babes don't toddle, they side-step. Queuing women talk of 'nipping round the blindside'. Rugby league provides our cultural adrenalin. It's a physical manifestation of our rules of life, comradeship, honest endeavour, and a staunch, often ponderous allegiance to fair play."
Writer **Colin Welland**

"We don't have stars in this game, that's soccer."
Frank Machin (**Richard Harris**) in the film, *This Sporting Life*

"Met Dad, went to Wembley. Played Chekhov in evening. Quite a day."
Hull-born actor **Sir Tom Courtenay** on the day the black and whites lost to Wigan in the 1959 Challenge Cup final

"Since I finished playing rugby league, apartheid has ended, the Iron Curtain has come down and the Israelis have given up the Gaza Strip to the Palestinians. But I still can't play rugby on a Saturday afternoon."
Former Castleford player **Ian Birkby**, who had been prevented from playing socially for a Cheshire rugby union club before the game went open

"I'm 49, I've had a brain hemorrhage and a triple bypass and I could still go out and play a reasonable game of rugby union. But I wouldn't last 30 seconds in rugby league."
Graham Lowe, the former Wigan and New Zealand coach

"League is much, much more physical than Union, and that's before anyone starts breaking the rules."
Former Welsh international rugby union player **Adrian Hadley** who went to play league with Salford

"It's the first time I've been cold for seven years. I was never cold playing rugby league."
Jonathan Davis, on the biggest change after returning to the union code

"The main difference between playing league and union is that now I get my hangovers on Monday instead of Sunday."
Former Welsh rugby union international **Tom David** after switching codes

"People had suggested that I count to ten when I had been riled. I tried but sometimes I didn't get past three!!"
One reason why **Jim Mills** was sent off around 20 times

"We had prepared to play George Foreman and got George Formby."
Brian Noble, the Bradford Bulls coach, on St Helens sending a drastically weakened team to Odsal

"We trained like Tarzan all week, then played like Jane."
Frank Endacott, the Widnes coaching adviser, after the Vikings' 40–6 hammering away to Wakefield Trinity Wildcats

"I'd rather be on Blackpool beach than Bondi beach."
Great Britain's **Leon Pryce** winds the locals up during the 2006 Tri Nations in Australia

— MOST POINTS IN A CAREER —

Neil Fox's career record 6,220 points consisted of 358 tries and 2,575 goals, including four one-point drop goals, in 828 matches. He was 16 when he made his senior debut for Wakefield Trinity and 40 when he played his last match, for Bradford Northern in 1979. At his peak he was a powerful top-class centre before moving into the pack.

Points	Scorer	Clubs	Career
6,220	Neil Fox	Wakefield Trinity, Bradford N, Hull KR, York, Bramley, Huddersfield	1956–79
6,022	Jim Sullivan	Wigan + (wartime) Dewsbury, Keighley, Bradford N.	1921–46
4,050	Gus Risman	Salford, Workington Town, Batley + (wartime) Dewsbury, Leeds, Hunslet, Bradford N.	1929–54
3,985	John Woods	Leigh, Bradford N., Warrington, Rochdale	1976–92
3,686	Cyril Kellett	Hull KR., Featherstone Rovers	1956–74
3,545	Kel Coslett	St Helens, Rochdale Hornets	1962–72
3,445	Lewis Jones	Leeds	1952–64
3,438	Steve Quinn	York, Featherstone Rovers	1970–88
3,381	Andrew Farrell	Wigan Warriors	1991–2004
3,279	Jim Ledgard	Leeds, Dewsbury, Leigh	1944–61

— RUGBY LEAGUE LEGENDS: TOM VAN VOLLENHOVEN —

The flying Springbok

Rugby League has seen many South Africans come to Britain and make their mark on the game but none have been as charismatic as the flying Springbok. Scorer of 392 tries in 409 matches for St Helens, Tom Van Vollenhoven was a classical winger with lightning pace, swerve and sidestep as well as being a terrific defence.

Born in Bethlehem in the Orange Free State in 1935, Van Vollenhoven proved a sensation when chosen for South Africa to play against the touring British Lions. Initially at centre, he subsequently moved to the wing and became the first Springbok to score a hat-trick in a Test in South Africa during the series. It has been suggested that the selectors didn't really know how to use his natural, instinctive talent and the following year he only played in the third Test while on a tour of New Zealand.

This snub may have prompted him to listen to offers from rugby league, with St Helens and Wigan leading the pack. The Saints eventually got him for a signing on fee of £4,000 but it was a desperately close thing. According to one of his St Helens team-mates, Ray French, Wigan missed out on signing him because the boy bringing the telegram to him with their offer was delayed after having to repair a puncture in one of the tyres of his bicycle.

Van Vollenhoven made his debut for St Helens against Leeds at Knowsley Road on 26th October 1957 in front of a crowd of 23,000 and registered his first try. His next game was in the 'A' team against Whitehaven which drew a remarkable crowd of 8,500.

The Springbok was a breath of fresh air to the team and with his smart crew cut and athletic frame he soon became a cult figure. Scoring freely, his balance was such that he often appeared to tiptoe down the touchline. One of his finest achievements was rescuing the Saints in the 1959 Championship final against Hunslet at Odsal with a hat-trick.

One of those tries is reputed to be the best he ever scored. Receiving the ball near his own line he jinked and sidestepped his way up the field past a succession of would-be tacklers before plonking the ball down at the other end. Although highlights of the game exist, it appears that the cameraman was having a break when this particular try was scored.

There were no such problems two years later when he

scored the try for which he will always be remembered against Wigan in the 1961 Challenge Cup final at Wembley. Once again it was a length of the field effort, but this time it involved a great inter-passing sequence with centre Ken Large. St Helens won 12–6 and he returned five years later to collect another winner's medal against the same opponents.

Van Vollenhoven retired in 1968, doing so in some style with a hat-trick against Wigan in his final appearance at Knowsley Road. He returned home to South Africa but such is his legendary status in St Helens that when he came back to the town in 1990 to take part in the club's centenary celebrations he spent three hours signing autographs for fans, many of whom weren't born when he played, queuing round the block to meet him.

He was inducted into the RFL's Hall of Fame in 2000 and in his native South Africa the local rugby league teams have named their competition the Tom Van Vollenhoven Cup in his honour.

Karel 'Tom' Van Vollenhoven
Born: 29th April 1935, Bethlehem, Orange Free State, South Africa
Position: Wing
Playing career: 1957–68
Club: St Helens
Scoring: 395 tries

— QUICKEST HAT-TRICK —

Chris Thorman of the Huddersfield Giants is credited with the fastest try hat-trick, completed within seven minutes of the kick-off. Playing at scrum half, he raced in for tries in the third, fifth and seventh minutes to help his side to a 45–30 win at the Doncaster Dragons in a Buddies National League Cup semi-final on 19th May 2002

— ON THE BOX —

Rugby League has popped up in television drama on many occasions. In the late 1970s Granada made a series called *Fallen Hero* about a Welsh rugby player who had gone north before being forced out of the game through injury. It starred Del Henney in the lead role as Gareth Hopkins, Wanda Ventham was the love interest and John Wheatley played Henney's brother. The series ran for seven episodes in 1978/79.

Where the Heart Is, which ran from 1997 until 2006, revolved around two sisters-in-law who were district nurses in the fictional Yorkshire town of Skelthwaite. One, Peggy, played by Pam Ferris, was married to Vic (Tony Haygarth) who was the ageing player/coach of the Skelthwaite Scorpions, an amateur rugby league team.

Legendary blonde bombshell Diana Dors starred as the manager of a rugby league team in a short-lived television series. Swindon-born Dors was cast as a Yorkshire matriarch in the series *Queenie's Castle* which was broadcast in the early 1970s.

When that came to an end Yorkshire TV came up with a new sitcom for her called *All Our Saturdays* in which she played the no-nonsense Di Dorkins – known as 'Big D' – who ran a large textile company, Garsley Garments, and managed the firm's amateur rugby league team, who she renamed the Frilly Things. It ran for six 30-minute episodes in 1973.

The popular soap *Emmerdale* featured a real life rugby league star in Martin Offiah, the former Great Britain winger, who appeared as himself in several episodes (alongside a non-speaking Gary Connolly). Offiah also appeared in a couple of episodes of *Hollyoaks*.

— LADIES TO THE RESCUE —

Rugby league players are tough but some of the women who follow the game are not to be trifled with either. In the 1966 Challenge Cup semi-final between St Helens and Dewsbury, John Warlow, the Saints Welsh forward, found himself the victim of a heavy tackle by Dewsbury's Dick Lowe.

Suddenly Warlow's landlady, Minnie Cotton, rushed on to the field and began attacking Lowe with her umbrella. Police and players eventually separated them and St Helens went on to win and book a place at Wembley. Minnie's husband George had been a St Helens player in the 1920s.

Solomon Haumono, the former Harlequins forward who gave up rugby league for boxing, was also involved in a bizarre on-field incident, while playing in Australia. After being left prone on the field following a heavy tackle, his mother ran on to the pitch to render assistance.

— POINTS IN A MATCH —

When George 'Tich' West scored his match record 11 tries for Hull Kingston Rovers against Brookland Rovers in 1905, he also kicked ten goals to give him a record 53 points. Remarkably, he kicked just one other goal that season and finished with a career total of only 44. Here's the full list of the highest individual scores in a single match:

Year	Points	Player	Opponents
1905	53	George West (Hull K.R.)	Brookland Rovers*
1925	44	Jim Sullivan (Wigan)	Flimby & Fothergill*
2005	44	Lee Birdseye (Rochdale Hornets)	Illingworth*
1973	43	Geoff 'Sammy' Lloyd (Castleford)	Millom*
1992	42	Dean Marwood (Workington Town)	Highfield
1994	42	Darren Carter (Barrow)	Nottingham City*
1995	42	Dean Marwood (Workington Town)	Leigh
1999	42	Iestyn Harris (Leeds Rhinos)	Huddersfield
2004	42	Neil Turley (Leigh Centurions)	Chorley Lynx
1986	40	Paul Loughlin (St Helens)	Carlisle
1992	40	Martin Offiah (Wigan)	Leeds
1992	40	Shaun Edwards (Wigan)	Swinton
1995	40	Martin Pearson (Featherstone)	Whitehaven
2000	40	Lee Briers (Warrington Wolves)	York
2001	40	Rob Burrow (England U-21s)	South Africa

* denotes amateur club

— THE CHALLENGE CUP: ORIGINS —

The most glittering prize in rugby league, the Challenge Cup has gained iconic status. It is the one rugby league event which has become part of the British sporting calendar and is relayed to an audience of millions on television both here and around the world.

The audience contains many millions who will never have seen a game live and never will, but as a sporting spectacle it remains unique. The match is shown throughout the world and even though it is in the middle of the night in Australia and New Zealand, countless players who come to play in Britain recount tales of getting up as kids to watch the match.

The newly formed Northern Union realised that cup competitions captured the imagination of the supporters and were great money-spinners. The Lancashire and Yorkshire cups had been particularly successful so they set about instigating a competition which would embrace all the clubs.

They called it the Challenge Cup and 52 clubs were involved in that first competition which was played during March and April 1897. The first final was between Batley and St Helens at Headingley and attracted a crowd of 13,492 (although 20,000 attended the semi-final between St Helens and Swinton).

The Yorkshire side won the final 10–3 and became the first team to lift the magnificent silver trophy which had been designed by a Bradford company Fattorini & Son. It weighed 189 ounces, stood three feet high and cost £60. Two sets of medals were also supplied.

The competition was a great success and soon the crowds for the finals were testing the capacities of the Northern grounds.

— TOP 10 SUPER LEAGUE CAREER GOALS —

Goals	Player	Years
979 (14)	Andrew Farrell (Wigan)	1996–2004
721 (17)	Paul Deacon (Bradford, Oldham)	1997–2006
683 (48)	Lee Briers (Warrington, St Helens)	1997–2006
613 (10)	Sean Long (St Helens, Wigan)	1996–2006
565 (8)	Iestyn Harris (Bradford, Leeds, Warrington)	1996–2006
526 (6)	Kevin Sinfield (Leeds)	1997–2006
511 (8)	Steve McNamara (Huddersfield, Wakefield, Bradford)	1997–2006
396 (5)	Henry Paul (Harlequins, Wigan, Bradford)	1996–2001, 06
371 (15)	Bobbie Goulding (Salford, Wakefield, Huddersfield, St Helens)	1996–2002
316 (3)	Paul Cooke (Hull)	1991–2006

Note: Stats correct up to and including season 2006. Drop goals included in total and shown in brackets.

— WARS OF THE ROSES —

Lancashire v Yorkshire matches were played annually from the inception of the Northern Union in 1895 until 1991. In 1985 the match was dubbed 'The War of the Roses' in an effort to spice up what was a flagging fixture but six years later it disappeared from the calendar.

In 2001 the clash was revived and in an effort to emulate the Australian State of Origin Series the match was called 'the Origin game' although the Lancashire team included London-born winger Dominic Peters who played for the London Broncos. The fixture was also promoted as a trial for the Great Britain Test team and a crowd of over 10,000, the biggest for a Lancashire/Yorkshire matches in 35 years, saw the red rose triumph 36–24.

The encounter became a two-game series over the next two years before being laid to rest once again.

— ODSAL'S BIG HOLE —

Odsal has been Bradford Northern's home since 1934 when a council tip and 140,000 cartloads of household waste had to be removed before it could be turned into a rugby league ground. But the fact that it was basically a huge hole in the ground was to make it unique.

The original dressing rooms were sited at the top of the terraces, which meant that the players had to stay on the pitch at half-time because it was so far to walk to get to them. Indeed after the final whistle the teams would find themselves threading through the departing crowds on their way to the changing rooms. The players' facilities have since been relocated to pitch level.

— THE LANCE TODD TROPHY —

The Lance Todd Trophy is presented to the Man of the Match at the Challenge Cup final. The winner is selected by the members of the Rugby League Writers' Association and is presented with the trophy at a celebratory dinner at The Willows, home of the Salford City Reds.

The trophy belongs to the Red Devils Association, the official body representing ex-Salford players, and it has been given to the Man of the Match in Challenge Cup finals since 1946. The trophy was inaugurated in memory of Lance Todd, the New Zealand-born player and administrator who was a member of the first Kiwi team to tour Britain. He later played for Wigan and became manager of Salford but was killed in a road accident in 1942.

The first winner was Wakefield's Billy Stott in 1946. Harry Sunderland, an Australian tour manager, broadcaster and journalist, was the driving force behind the introduction of the award and 20 years later his name was also given to the Man of the Match award for the best player in the Championship final, later Super League's Grand Final.

In 2006, St Helens scrum half Sean Long became the first player in the history of Rugby League to be awarded the Lance Todd Trophy on three separate occasions. His Man of the Match performance against Huddersfield at Twickenham followed similar feats against Bradford (2001) and Wigan (2004).

— LONDON CALLING: PART ONE —

There have been numerous attempts to establish rugby league in the capital. Moving the Challenge Cup final to Wembley in 1929 was a huge gamble which paid off but establishing the game in London has proved more difficult.

In 1932 Leeds played Wigan in an exhibition match at the White City Stadium in west London under floodlights. The stadium authorities were impressed enough to take over the Wigan Highfield club and relocate it to their stadium. They played a season as London Highfield, home games were on Wednesday nights under floodlights and although they finished mid-table with crowds of 5–7,000 they lost money having to pay visiting clubs travelling expenses. The venture failed and in the following season the club moved back up North again to become Liverpool Stanley.

However another sports promoter, Sydney Parkes, formed two teams, Acton & Willesden and Streatham & Mitcham, to play at his dog track in Mitcham. They entered the rugby league for the 1935/36 season but the Acton venture only lasted one season.

Streatham, however, looked well set after having recruited some star players including the legendary New Zealander George Nepia and attracting average gates of 10,000 but they disbanded in March 1937.

— FASTEST GOAL —

Quite a few goals have been kicked after a side was penalised at the kick-off, but the most famous came at the start of the 1965 Challenge Cup final at Wembley. Wigan's Laurie Gilfedder landed it from the centre spot after the kick-off by Hunslet half back Alan Marchant went straight into touch. Gilfedder's mighty kick sent the ball soaring over the bar after just 54 seconds. It was to prove an important score as underdogs Hunslet gave the red hot favourites a nervous time before going down 20–16.

— RUGBY LEAGUE LEGENDS: MAL MENINGA —

Aussie legend Mal Meninga

That Mal Meninga has made more appearances and scored more points than any other Australian player tells only half the story of this extraordinary player. A giant 16 stone centre with deceptive speed and great hands, he was one of the game's biggest stars in the 1980s and early 1990s and in one short spell with St Helens achieved legendary status within the town.

Meninga was born in Bundaberg in Queensland and is of Samoan descent, which goes some way to explain his massive frame. He began his career in Brisbane at the age of 18 with Souths Magpies, winning two Brisbane Premierships with them in 1981 and 1985. In 1980 he featured in the first State of Origin match, helping Queensland in their victory over New South Wales by kicking seven goals from seven attempts with his old-fashioned toe end kicking style. He joined St Helens for their 1984/85 campaign during the Australian off-season for a reputed £30,000 and helped them to Lancashire Cup and Premiership triumphs

In 1986, Meninga joined the Canberra Raiders in the New South Wales Rugby League competition and led them to their first Premiership in 1989, beating the Balmain Tigers in the Grand Final. He followed that up the next year with another grand final victory against the Penrith Panthers. Fittingly Meninga played his last game for the Canberra Raiders in the 1994 Grand Final where he led his team to victory over the Canterbury Bulldogs, their third Premiership in six years, scoring the last try of the match.

He captained Australia for 23 Test matches between 1990 and 1994, and led the Queensland State of Origin team for three years from 1992 to 1994. Meninga is the only player to captain a Kangaroo tour party on two occasions, in 1990 and 1994. On 4th December 1994 at Béziers, France, he captained Australia to a 74–0 victory over the French, scoring the final try of the game, and of his career.

The main grandstand at Bruce Stadium in Canberra is named the Mal Meninga stand in his honour. Meninga was appointed coach of the Raiders in 1997 but achieved only moderate success. In 2000 he was awarded the Australian Sports Medal for his contribution to Australia's international standing in rugby league. The following year he received the Centenary Medal "for services as a role model and inspiration as a rugby league player of the highest standard".

He was appointed coach of the Queensland State of Origin team in 2006.

Malcolm Norman Meninga
Born: 8th July 1960 in Bundaberg, Queensland
Position: Centre
Playing career: 1978–1984
Clubs: South's Magpies (Aus), St Helens (UK), Canberra Raiders (Aus)
International record: Australia (47 apps, 21 tries, 102 goals)
Scoring: 242 tries, 882 goals, 2 drop goals

— POINTS IN A SEASON —

When Lewis Jones scored his record 496 points in 1956/57 the only time he failed to score in 48 club and representative matches was in the last game of the season, Leeds' 9–7 defeat of Barrow in the Challenge Cup final at Wembley. His best match feat during the season was a then club record 31 points against Bradford Northern.

Points	Scorer	Club	Season
496	Lewis Jones	(Leeds)	1956–57
493	David Watkins	(Salford)	1972–73
490	John Wasyliw	(Keighley C.)	1992–93
481	Andrew Farrell	(Wigan Warriors)	2001
476	David Watkins	(Salford)	1971–72
468	Neil Turley	(Leigh C.)	2004
457	Henry Paul	(Bradford Bulls)	2001
456	Neil Fox	(Wakefield Tr.)	1961–62
453	Bernard Ganley	(Oldham)	1957–58
453	Neil Fox	(Wakefield Tr.)	1959–60

— HIGHEST SCORES —

Huddersfield scored 26 tries when they thrashed Blackpool Gladiators 142–4 on 26th November 1994, setting a domestic scoring record in the process.

Greg Austin led the try-scoring with nine and Dean Hanger – a substitute – got five. Phil Hellewell kicked 12 goals and Laurent Lucchese hit seven. The previous record points total, 119 also by Huddersfield, had lasted 80 years. But the old record included 27 tries, then worth only three points.

Score	Game	Date
142–4	**Huddersfield** v Blackpool Gladiators	26th November 1994
138–0	**Barrow** v Nottingham City	27th November 1994
120–4	**Rochdale Hornets** v Illingworth	13th March 2005
119–2	**Huddersfield** v Swinton Park	28th February 1914
116–0	**Wigan** v Flimby & Fothergill	14th February 1925
112–0	**St Helens** v Carlisle	14th September 1986
106–10	Swinton Lions v **Leeds Rhinos**	11th February 2001
104–12	**St Helens** v Trafford Borough	15th September 1991
104–4	**Keighley Cougars** v Highfield	23rd April 1995
102–0	**Leeds** v Coventry	12th April 1913

— SUPER LEAGUE RECORDS: PART ONE —

*Andy Farrell: More points in a single
season than any other player*

Most tries in a match: 6 by Lesley Vainikolo (Bradford Bulls)
v Hull FC, 2nd September 2005
Lesley Vainikolo's Super League record six tries against Hull
began a try-scoring run that brought him 16 in only five

matches. The big Bradford Bulls winger followed his record-breaking feat with two each against Huddersfield Giants, St Helens and London Broncos before completing the sequence with another four against Hull.

Most goals in a match: 14 by Henry Paul (Bradford Bulls) v Salford City Reds, 25th June 2000

When Henry Paul kicked his Super League record 14 goals he also scored a try and his brother, Robbie, got four touchdowns. That gave the Paul brothers a total of 48 points, exactly half the score in Bradford Bulls' club record 96–16 defeat of Salford City Reds.

Most points in a match: 42 (13 goals, four tries) by Iestyn Harris (Leeds Rhinos) v Huddersfield Giants, 16th July 1999

Iestyn Harris's Super League record 42 points also beat the Leeds record of 31 set by the legendary Lewis Jones in 1956. Jones had left Welsh rugby union and went on to score a career record 2,920 for Leeds. Ironically, Harris was almost halfway to that target when he left for Welsh rugby union.

Most tries in a season: 36 by Lesley Vainikolo (Bradford Bulls), 2004

Lesley Vainikolo rattled up his record-breaking 36 tries in only 24 matches. He failed to touch down in only seven matches in which he played. Vainikolo started with a then Super League record-equalling five tries against Wigan Warriors in the opening match. The New Zealand Test winger went on to score four other hat-tricks, including one four-try feat.

Most goals in a season: 168 by Henry Paul (Bradford Bulls), 2001

Henry Paul's record 168 goals included a run of 25 successive successful kicks over four rounds of Super League. His best match feat during the season was 11 goals. Twice he kicked ten in a match. The New Zealander's season total included three drop goals.

Most points in a season : 388 by Andrew Farrell (Wigan Warriors), 2001
Andrew Farrell's record 388 points consisted of 16 tries and 164 goals, including four drop goals. Five times he scored 20 points or more in a match with a best tally of 30 from two tries and 11 goals. He particularly enjoyed himself against Leeds Rhinos as he piled up 56 points in three matches.

Scored in every round: Andrew Farrell (Wigan Warriors) 23 matches in 1998 and 28 matches in 2001.

Note: These records do not include play-off games.

— THE WORLD CUP: THE 1960s —

The third World Cup was due to be held in 1965 but the Australians called it off because they didn't think the French would be competitive having lost all three Test matches on their tour there the previous year.

In 1968 there was to be a bona fide final between the teams finishing first and second in the table after all the sides had played each other. It was also the first time that the competition was spread over two countries, New Zealand and Australia, and the first to be played under a limited (four) tackle rule. France surprised everyone by finishing runners-up to Australia, after losing to the co-hosts in the final played at the Sydney Cricket Ground.

— WHAT'S IN A NAME —

The advent of Super League prompted many clubs to adopt American-style marketing techniques. Most disregarded their old nicknames and added new more marketable ones, although you will still hear fans on the terraces shout for 'The Wire' or 'Fartown'.

Bradford Northern became the Bulls, Castleford known for years simply as 'Cas' became the Tigers, Halifax changed from being plain 'Fax' to the Blue Sox but have since reverted back to their original name. Leeds were called the Loiners, although few people outside Headingley knew what a Loiner was, so not surprisingly they became the more user-friendly Rhinos. Even more obscure, Oldham were and still are the Roughyeds although during their brief Super League sojourn they became the Bears. Warrington were known as 'The Wire', a reference to the local wire industry, but they're now the Wolves. Similarly, the Widnes nickname 'the Chemics' reflected the local chemical industry. They're now the Vikings although an element of their old name lives on in their mascot, called Kemik the Viking.

Wigan, or anyone from the town, may be universally referred to as 'pie eaters' but with the advent of Super League they became Warriors. The Red Devils of Salford decided to revel in their city status and became the City Reds and although Huddersfield are now the Giants and play in a posh new stadium you will still hear fans shout for 'Fartown', the name of their old ground. Still it's better than the Barracudas, which is what they called themselves briefly in the mid-1980s.

Hull became the Sharks briefly but to distinguish them from the club from the other side in the city, Hull Kingston Rovers are referred to as FC, which is normally used by soccer clubs. St Helens and Workington Town have resisted all temptation to add a fancy name, although the Australian media once referred to St Helens as the St Helens Saints!

— WIDE TO WEST —

Rugby league's pre-eminence as a handling game has produced many great tries and to attempt to pick out the best is virtually impossible. However, there is one remarkable touchdown which lives in the memory of all those who saw it.

In the Super League era, St Helens have been adept at snatching victory from the jaws of defeat, but even by their standards the try they scored against the Bradford Bulls on 22nd September 2000 was something special. The Saints had finished second in the table, just one place above Bradford, which gave them home advantage against the Bulls in this play-off game at Knowsley Road.

However, they trailed 11–10 with just three seconds to go and when Paul Sculthorpe played the ball in the left-hand corner of the pitch 25 metres from his own line, the game seemed lost. But the final play of the game was a stunning example of Saints' never-say-die attitude.

Keiron Cunningham, the hooker, passed to Sean Long and the scrum half sent a speculative kick across the field to the opposite wing. It wasn't deep enough for the wide players to chase, indeed it was more of a chip, probably looking to stretch the Bradford defence. It was taken by Kevin Iro who fed Steve Hall and the wingman, realising that he had to keep the ball alive, passed inside to Sean Hoppe. Hoppe flicked it over his shoulder back to Hall and on to Tim Jonkers who returned the ball to Long, the scrum half having moved in to the centre of the pitch.

Saints were probing for an opening and, as the hooter had already sounded, knew they had to keep the ball alive because as soon as the play was halted either by a tackle, an error or the ball going out of play then that would be the end of the game. Despite all their efforts thus far they actually hadn't made any progress upfield.

Suddenly Long injected some pace into the proceedings,

sprinting towards the left-hand touchline where he found second row Chris Joynt in the centre position. Joynt shipped the ball on to Dwayne West on the wing, a player whose career was blighted by injury and who would only play a handful of games for the club. This was to prove one of his most memorable.

The match was being shown live on Sky Sports and commentator Eddie Hemmings, sensing the mounting tension, shrieked: "It's wide to West, it's wide to West!". The Bradford defence, though, looked to have things under control and refused to be drawn into making a rash tackle. However, West suddenly kicked out of a despairing Bradford tackle and was free down the left.

The Bulls full back Michael Withers moved across to snuff out the danger but Joynt, the St Helens skipper, found enough in his weary legs to support West on the inside. As Withers closed in on West, he turned the ball inside to Joynt who by this time was well inside the Bradford half.

Anthony Sullivan, a wingman with real pace who would later play rugby union for Wales, burst through in support but Joynt knew he had the legs to go all the way and wasn't about to take the risk of making another pass. After raising one arm in salute, he crossed the line and plonked the ball down.

The crowd erupted and Bradford coach Matthew Elliott was so stunned he fell off his seat in the stand and disappeared from view. Long was so overcome with joy that he decided to celebrate by plucking the giant head off the St Bernard mascot and putting it on before trotting round the field.

He was eventually persuaded to take it off to kick the conversion, which gave his team a 16–11 victory. After this amazing performance nothing was going to stop Saints on their way to the Grand Final at Old Trafford where they beat the Wigan Warriors 29–16.

— RUGBY LEAGUE LEGENDS: BILLY BOSTON —

Billy Boston: Wigan's great Welshman

Billy Boston was one of the greatest players even to wear a Wigan jersey. A blockbusting winger of tremendous power and strength he was probably the greatest Welsh rugby player never to play for his country at rugby union.

Boston was born in the Tiger Bay area of Cardiff in 1934, the son of a father from Sierra Leone and an Irish mother.

He had already attracted attention in youth rugby, he was already over 12 and a half stones, but it was when he began his National Service with the Army at Catterick in 1952 that he really caused a stir.

Playing rugby union for a star-studded Royal Corps of Signals team his scoring feats were sensational and after claiming six tries in a cup final against the Welsh Guards, Wigan signed him on Friday 13th March 1953 for £3,000.

He made his debut in October, when 8,500 turned up at Central Park to see him score a couple of tries for the 'A' team against Barrow. Three weeks later Barrow were again the opponents when he made his first team debut, when he scored the first of many tries.

After barely a handful of games for the club he was selected for the Great Britain tour to Australia in 1954, becoming the first black British player to tour. He rewarded that early leap of faith by becoming the leading try scorer with 36, a record which included four in the first Test against New Zealand in Auckland.

By the end of the tour he had filled out to over 14 stones but it wasn't just his power which made him such devastating winger. He was quick, could sidestep and swerve and possessed a fierce hand-off which made tackling him a daunting prospect.

Although he became heavier as he got older, Boston retained all his impressive attributes. With Wigan he couldn't stop scoring, twice notching up seven tries in a match, against Dewsbury and Salford. He appeared in six Wembley finals, collecting a winner's medal on three occasions and played in the 1957 World Cup for Great Britain and toured again in 1962.

Although rugby league has always prided itself on embracing players from all backgrounds and cultures, it was while coming back from that 1957 World Cup tournament that Boston experienced one of the worst examples of racial discrimination. The Great Britain team had agreed to play

some exhibition games in South Africa on the way home –
however, with the country in the grip of apartheid, instead
of taking part in the games, Boston was flown directly home
on his own.

He played his last match for Wigan against Wakefield
Trinity in April 1968, having scored 478 tries in his
15 seasons with them. In common with the only man to
score more tries than him, Brian Bevan, he had a couple
of seasons with Blackpool Borough before retiring with a
total of 571 tries for club and country. For many years
Boston ran a pub in Wigan, The Griffin, across the road
from Central Park where he had scored so many of his
tries. He was inducted into the Rugby Football League's
Hall of Fame in 1988.

William John Boston
Born: 6th August 1934, Cardiff
Position: Wing
Playing career: 1953–70
Clubs: Wigan, Blackpool Borough
International record: Great Britain (31 apps, 24 tries)
Scoring: 571 tries, 7 goals

— ANOTHER BLOODY SUNDAY —

In 1981 a Yorkshire Television documentary followed the
fortunes of Doncaster Rovers rugby league club, whose run
of defeats had earned them a place in the Guinness Book
of Records. Called *Another Bloody Sunday* the cameras
followed the players and the committee as they struggled to
cope both on and off the pitch. It was shown again on
Channel 4 in 1992.

— MOST TRAVELLED —

The team originally known as Wigan Highfield are the rugby league club who have had the most varied incarnations. Originally formed as a rugby union club in 1880 they went out of existence for a few years following the great split of 1895. They reformed in 1902 and played in a league comprising the 'A' teams of the major clubs.

In 1922 they entered the main competition and their first game was a local derby against Wigan. In 1933, they finished second from bottom in the league and the owners of the White City Stadium in London, who saw rugby league as a way of generating new income for their stadium, bought the club and renamed them London Highfield.

However that venture only lasted a year and in 1934 they returned north to the Stanley greyhound stadium in Liverpool and became Liverpool Stanley. In 1935/36 Stanley won the Lancashire League. For the start of the 1950/51 season the club moved to Mill Yard, Knotty Ash and was renamed Liverpool City. In 1956 they hosted the touring Australian national team, losing 40–12 in front of a crowd of over 4,700.

In July 1964 the club's board were informed that the Knotty Ash lease would not be renewed and negotiations then took place with the local authority in nearby Huyton for a 21-year lease at Alt Park which was eventually ready in August 1969. Alt Park, though, was of poor standard and often suffered from vandalism.

The club continued as Huyton RLFC and struggled in the Second Division until 1985, when they moved to Canal Street, Runcorn, home of Runcorn football club which precipitated another change of name to Runcorn Highfield. When Highfield drew Wigan at home in the John Player Trophy on 13th November 1988, the club's supporters saw it as an ideal opportunity to persuade the people of Runcorn to come and give Highfield a try. However, the directors had the game switched to Central Park in exchange for a fee from Wigan, on the grounds that Canal Street did not have the capacity.

The players, seeing that the club would receive more money, asked for a greater share of the takings. However, the directors refused, leading to a mass player strike. The team that faced Wigan comprised a number of trialists and reserves together with the coach, Bill Ashurst, who had come out of retirement. Highfield lost 92–2 in front of a crowd of 7,233 at Central Park and Ashurst was sent off after 11 minutes. The club never seemed to recover from this blow, and they went on to lose every game in the 1989/90 season, finishing eight points behind second bottom club Nottingham City.

They were soon on the move again, to another football club, St Helens Town and in August 1990 they moved to the club's Hoghton Road ground in the Sutton area of the town and began the 1991/92 season as simply Highfield.

This latest move prompted an upturn in fortunes. They finished 14th out of 20 clubs in the Second Division, and reached the second round of the Challenge Cup. Two years later they managed 11th place, finishing above such teams as Fulham, Huddersfield, Workington Town and Keighley. However, they struggled to attract more than a few hundred spectators to their games.

The 1994/95 season was a disaster for Highfield. They won only two games all season – against amateurs Ovenden 12–6 in the first round of the Regal Trophy and against Barrow 14–12 in the league. They lost to amateurs Beverley 27–4 in the Challenge Cup and their final home game was on 17th April 1995 when they lost 34–8 to Barrow in front of a crowd of just 195.

Their final game (played at Rochdale Hornets ground on 23rd April 1995) was a humiliating 104–4 defeat by Keighley Cougars. Needless to say they finished bottom of the Second Division having conceded a grand total of 1,604 points in 30 league games.

Despite all this Highfield survived into the Super League

era but fared even worse in the 1995/96 season gaining just one point all season (a 24–24 draw against York), their only win coming against amateurs Hemel Hempstead in the first round of the Regal Trophy. Their final game was a 82–0 defeat away at Hunslet on 21st January 1996 and another move, their last, was on the cards.

They relocated to Hope Street in Prescot, home of local football team Prescot Cables and were renamed Prescot Panthers for the start of the 1996 season. They won just two games and struggled on for the 1997 season, again winning two games, but bowed to the inevitable and resigned from the league at the end of the season. Ironically the club's final game was a 72–10 defeat by Carlisle, who were also playing their final league game. Prescot finished at the bottom for a fifth successive season. Chairman Geoff Fletcher accepted a one-off payment of around £30,000 for the club to resign from the Rugby Football League, which they duly did.

— TOP 10 SUPER LEAGUE CAREER POINTS —

Points	Player	Years
2,228	Andrew Farrell (Wigan)	1996–2004
1,657	Paul Deacon (Bradford, Oldham)	1997–2006
1,628	Sean Long (St Helens, Wigan)	1996–2006
1,590	Lee Briers (Warrington, St Helens)	1997–2006
1,458	Iestyn Harris (Bradford, Leeds, Warrington)	1996–2006
1,174	Kevin Sinfield (Leeds)	1997–2006
1,090	Steve McNamara (Huddersfield, Wakefield, Bradford)	1996–2003
1,035	Henry Paul (Harlequins, Wigan, Bradford)	1996–2001 & 2006–
974	Paul Sculthorpe (St Helens, Warrington)	1996–2006
897	Danny Orr (Wigan, Castleford)	1997–2006

Note: Stats correct up to and including season 2006.

— RUGBY APARTHEID —

The great split of 1895 sparked one of the longest running feuds in sport. The southern-based RFU never forgave the northern rebels and over the next 100 years did their damnedest to kill off rugby league and ostracise anyone associated with it.

It was only in 1995, when rugby union finally acknowledged that players of their own game were being paid and offered inducements, that they were forced to go open. Players and coaches could now go from one sport to the other, but some of the things that had happened during that century of vilification still leave league followers very bitter.

For the majority of those 100 years, any rugby union player knowingly taking part in a match involving someone who had played, coached or been involved in rugby league, could be banned from the sport for life. Up until 1987, even if you played amateur rugby league you weren't allowed to play union.

It was said that a murderer could play for the prison rugby union team, but an inmate who had played rugby league could not. Only in the armed forces were league players allowed to play union.

The discrimination began immediately after the split and some of the stories often beggar belief. In the first season of the Northern Union, for example, the Huddersfield Police played a union match against the 'Old Fossils' to raise money to buy a horse ambulance for the borough. Because the match had taken place at Fartown, home to Northern Union side Huddersfield, the Rugby Football Union declared that all the policemen had professionalised themselves and were consequently banned.

Ben Gronow, a Welsh rugby union international who had gone north to play league with Huddersfield, became coach of Morley rugby union club in the 1930s. However, when the club published a brochure on its history he was identified as 'unknown' on a team photograph, hardly likely since he was the first man to kick-off an international at Twickenham.

The story of Ronnie Cowan is even more ridiculous. A Scotland union international in the early 1960s, he played league for Leeds before returning home. Cowan coached the local union club Selkirk but, because he was not allowed to set foot on the pitch, had to do so from behind a hedge which ran parallel to the touchline.

Broadcaster Ray French became an England rugby union international while playing for St Helens rugby union club. After playing league for St Helens, Widnes and Great Britain he began coaching his old union club until it became public. He was banned from coaching, prevented from entering clubhouses and, despite being a schoolmaster, the union authorities even tried to stop him coaching schools rugby.

George Parsons, who became the youngest-ever rugby union forward to be capped by Wales, was thrown off a train taking the Welsh team to France on suspicion of having been approached by a league club. He eventually signed for St Helens for whom he played 296 matches and had to wait 34 years to receive his Welsh rugby union cap.

But it wasn't just players who found themselves ostracized and thrown out of clubhouses. In the 1959 general election the former Conservative cabinet minister Michael Jopling was fighting the Wakefield constituency as a Tory candidate. He was invited to kick- off the Wakefield Trinity v Hunslet rugby league match which he thought would be good for his campaign, given that around 15,000 local electors would be present. However, Jopling was subsequently banned from rugby union indefinitely for having 'professionalised' himself.

Union players who fancied switching codes would often play trials for a league club, usually in the 'A' team. To preserve their anonymity they were put down as

A.N. Other or S.O. Else and many went back to playing rugby union.

David Hinchcliffe, who became MP for Wakefield in 1987, campaigned tirelessly for an end to the hypocrisy and was a leading light in the all-party Rugby League Group. He highlighted the case of Steve Pilgrim, a three-quarter with Wasps who was banned after being spotted playing in a trial with Leeds for which he received no money.

Similarly Adrian Spencer, who played for Cambridge in the Varsity Match, was banned after it was revealed that he had also had a few games for the London Crusaders, without being paid.

Yet rugby union had been regularly tainted with accusations of players being paid. There was the famous boot money scandal in the 1970s when international players were paid to wear a particular manufacturer's boots. Mike Catt, the England international, admitted receiving £140 a week in expenses when he played in his native South Africa but nothing was done about it. In France, rugby union clubs often poached rugby league players, waving away criticism by saying that league clubs were all amateur in France anyway.

Even considering an offer to turn professional could land a union player in hot water. When Wales and Lions wing J.J. Williams, admitted in a newspaper that he had been offered £16,000 by Widnes just before he was due play for Llanelli against Swansea. Williams was told he had 'professionalised' himself and wasn't allowed to play in the match.

Thankfully all that is now in the past, but many league followers have long memories.

— GOALS IN A SEASON —

David Watkins had never been a serious goal kicker during his illustrious rugby union career in Wales. And it was almost three years after signing for Salford that he took over the role. Then he quickly became a record breaker. Within three years he had broken the season record and went on to set a Salford career best of 1,241 goals

Here's a list of the top 10 highest goalscorers in a single season, including drop goals:

Goals	Scorer	Club	Season
221	David Watkins	(Salford)	1972–73
219	Bernard Ganley	(Oldham)	1957–58
214	Kel Coslett	(St Helens)	1971–72
213	Henry Paul	(Bradford Bulls)	2001
207	Andrew Farrell	(Wigan Warriors)	2000
199	Mike Fletcher	(Hull KR)	1989–90
194	Jim Sullivan	(Wigan)	1933–34
194	Lewis Jones	(Leeds)	1956–57
193	Kel Coslett	(St Helens)	1970–71
193	David Watkins	(Salford)	1971–72

— THE HARRY SUNDERLAND AWARD —

It wasn't until 1965 that a man of the match award was made to the best player in the Championship final. It was named after Harry Sunderland, an Australian who was tour manager of the 1929, 1933 and 1937 Kangaroos.

With the move to two division football in 1973, the trophy was awarded at the Premiership final. Today it is given to the outstanding player in the Super League Grand Final as judged by the rugby league writers.

— THE CHALLENGE CUP:
THE WEMBLEY YEARS, PART ONE —

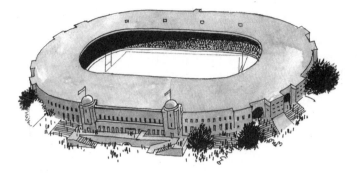

Following the suggestion of a John Leake, who presided over a dozen amateur rugby league clubs in South Wales, the Rugby Football League considered taking the Challenge Cup final to London.

Wembley, or the Empire Stadium as it was called then, wasn't the automatic choice as both White City and Crystal Palace were also in the running. However the Twin Towers got the vote and the first final was played there on 4th May 1929 between Dewsbury and Wigan.

Wigan won 13–2 in front of 41,500, the second highest crowd ever for a Challenge Cup final, but the massive increase in receipts meant that Wembley was to become a fixture in the rugby league calendar despite some attempts in the ensuing years to take it back up north.

When, due to the early departure of the Great Britain touring team, the final clashed with the FA Cup final in 1932 the final was played at Wigan. But a disappointing crowd meant that the arguments for taking future finals up north were not heard again.

Apart from the war years, Wembley hosted the final until 1999 when it was knocked down and rebuilt. The Challenge Cup final became not just a day out for the supporters of the two finalists but an annual pilgrimage for all rugby league folk. Some of the game's greatest matches and most spectacular tries were seen on Challenge Cup day at Wembley.

The 1949 clash between Bradford Northern and Halifax saw the first ever capacity attendance of 95,050. The first draw at Wembley in 1954 between Halifax and Warrington resulted in the biggest ever attendance for a rugby match at Odsal for the replay.

The 1961 final between St Helens and Wigan saw one of the greatest tries when South African wing Tom Van Vollenhoven went the length of the field interpassing with centre Ken Large in scorching heat to score a try in their 12–6 victory.

Five years later the two teams were back again in front of a record attendance of 98,536 as the Saints again beat their bitter rivals 21–6. One of the biggest upsets, meanwhile, was the triumph of an Alex Murphy-inspired Leigh over Leeds 24–7 in 1971.

— TRIES IN A CAREER —

Brian Bevan was a try-scoring freak. His career record 796 tries came in 688 matches. Among his other records was a century of hat-tricks, including a Warrington best of seven in a match – twice. He also holds the Warrington records for tries in a season (66) and in a career (740). Liverpool Stanley suffered the most as he scored 69 against them.

Here's a list of the top 10 highest try scorers in English rugby league history:

Tries	Player	Clubs	Career
796	Brian Bevan	Warrington, Blackpool Borough	1945–64
571	Billy Boston	Wigan, Blackpool Borough	1953–70
481	Martin Offiah	Widnes, Wigan, London Broncos, Salford City Reds	1987–2005
446	Alf Ellaby	St Helens, Wigan	1926–39
443	Eric Batten	Wakefield Trinity, Hunslet, Bradford Northern, Featherstone Rovers + (wartime) Dewsbury, Leeds, Castleford, Huddersfield	1933–54
441	Lionel Cooper	Huddersfield	1947–55
428	Ellery Hanley	Bradford Northern, Wigan, Leeds	1978– 95
415	Johnny Ring	Wigan, Rochdale Hornets	1922–33
406	Clive Sullivan	Hull, Hull K.R., Oldham, Doncaster	1961–85
401	John Atkinson	Leeds, Carlisle	1966–83

— GOING NORTH —

Wales has always been a fertile recruiting ground for rugby league. Even before the split of 1895 there was a steady flow of players joining northern clubs but with the advent of professionalism the move became even more attractive.

The economic depression in the 1920s hit south Wales particularly hard so it wasn't surprising that this decade saw more Welshmen 'going north' to play rugby league than any other. By the 1922/23 season there were up to 50 Welshmen playing in the newly titled Rugby Football League.

Decade	Turned Pro
1890s	12
1900s	9
1910s	18
1920s	37
1930s	27
1940s	6
1950s	7
1960s	14
1970s	6
1980s	11
1990s	7
Total	**154**

— TEETHING TROUBLES —

An Australian rugby league player competed for 15 weeks unaware that an opponent's tooth was buried in his forehead. Prop Ben Czislowski, 24, had played in the NRL with the Brisbane Broncos and the Canterbury Bulldogs before dropping down a level.

In a game for Brisbane club Wynnum against Tweed Heads on 1st April 2007, he clashed heads with opposite number Matt Austin. Czislowski had the resulting wound stitched up but subsequently suffered from an eye infection and complained of shooting pains in his head and feeling lethargic.

A visit to his doctor in mid-July revealed a tooth imbedded in his head. After having it removed he said, "I can laugh about it now, but the doctor told me it could have been serious with teeth carrying germs." Czislowski kept the tooth as a souvenir.

But this wasn't an isolated incident. In 2004, Australian hooker Shane Millard also had an opponent's tooth removed from his head, which he'd picked up while playing for the Widnes Vikings in Super League. Millard subsequently played for the Leeds Rhinos and the Wigan Warriors.

In 2002 another Australian, Jamie Ainscough was playing for Wigan when he began having problems with his arm. It became so badly infected that there were fears it might have to be amputated. Eventually an x-ray revealed an imbedded tooth. It apparently belonged to Warrington centre Martin Gleeson who Ainscough had played against a month before.

— THIS SPORTING LIFE —

This Sporting Life is the best film ever made on rugby league. Based on the novel written by Wakefield-born David Storey and published in 1960, it was made into a film starring Richard Harris and directed by Lindsay Anderson and released in 1963.

Storey, himself a former professional league player, also wrote the screenplay. Anderson chose the Yorkshire town because he had shot four documentaries in the area and by coincidence Trinity were the best team in rugby league at that time.

The film tells the story of Frank Machin, a coal miner who goes to lodge with a widow, played by Rachel Roberts and her two children. Machin has trials for the local rugby league team and is signed by them. The story centres around his brutal world on the pitch and his fractious relationship with his landlady off it.

The film was nominated for Academy Awards for Best

Actor in a Leading Role (Richard Harris) and Best Actress in a Leading Role (Rachel Roberts). It boasts an impressive cast of great British actors including Alan Badel, Colin Blakely, Jack Watson, George Sewell, Vanda Godsell and Arthur Lowe, many of whom went on to greater things.

Arthur Lowe appeared in *Coronation Street* but is probably best known for his performances as Captain Mainwaring in *Dad's Army*. Among the supporting cast was William Hartnell, who plays the scout Johnson. It was his performance in the film which brought Hartnell to the attention of Verity Lambert, the producer of the classic children's science fiction series *Doctor Who*. Hartnell became the very first Doctor.

Frank Windsor, who starred in *Z Cars* and *Softly Softly*, plays a dentist who works on Machin's teeth after he's been stiff-armed and Leonard Rossiter, later to gain fame in *Rising Damp* and *The Fall and Rise Of Reginald Perrin* features as a local sports reporter while Glenda Jackson makes an unnamed appearance.

Many of the scenes were filmed in and around Wakefield with all the action sequences shot at Trinity's Belle Vue stadium, although one scene after a game takes place at Halifax's old Thrum Hall ground. The film featured many Wakefield players including their real life coach Ken Traill.

This Sporting Life was part of a film movement known as the British new wave which specialised in gritty, working class stories as portrayed in *Saturday Night and Sunday Morning* and *A Taste of Honey*. Although not a commercial success at the time it has become quite a cult classic given the later successes of Harris and Anderson, who went on to direct *If* and *O Lucky Man*.

The rugby scenes are considered some of the best sporting images ever filmed. Storey later returned to the rugby theme with a play called *The Changing Room*.

— THE ALL GOLDS —

By breaking away from the Rugby Football Union in 1895, the players and officials of the newly formed Northern Union cut themselves off from international competition. Although a number of games were staged in the early years between an England team and a side of Other Nationalities (essentially Welshmen and a few Scots), it wasn't a true international fixture.

Indeed, it is possible that rugby league would never have become much more than a northern oddity if it hadn't been for a postal clerk from Wellington, New Zealand. Albert Henry Baskerville was a 24 year old forward with the Oriental rugby club who had even written a book on the sport *Modern Rugby Football: New Zealand Methods; Points for the Beginner, the Player, the Spectator.*

However, he followed with interest the activities of the Northern Union and saw a commercial opportunity. He contacted the union to see if they would be willing to host a touring party and then got together with George Smith, who had toured Britain with the All Blacks in 1905, and recruited 26 New Zealand players for a tour of England and Wales in 1907/08 to be played under Northern Union rules.

Nicknamed the 'All Golds', a mocking reference to the money-driven nature of the venture, the tourists included eight former All Blacks. However, before heading for the British Isles they called into Australia, playing three games under union laws against new South Wales in Sydney. As a result Australia's star player, Dally Messenger, was persuaded to join the tour.

The 'All Golds' landed at Folkstone in September 1907 and played their first game against Bramley on 9th October, winning 25–6. The first ever game of international rugby league took place on 1st January 1908 at the New Athletic Grounds, Aberdare when the tourists lost 9–8 to Wales.

However, they went on to win the three-match Test series against England, losing at Headingley before winning the second at Chelsea and the third at Cheltenham. In 35 matches the 'All Golds' won 19 and drew two, not bad for a team who had never played under Northern Union rules before arriving in Britain. Ten of the touring team stayed on to play for Northern Union clubs, starting a tradition of imported Australian and New Zealand talent which continues today.

International rugby league was born but its creator, Henry Baskerville never got to see it develop. He contracted pneumonia on the way home and died in Brisbane on 20th May 20 1908.

That first tour was commemorated in the autumn of 2007 when New Zealand contested a three-match Test series in Great Britain. In a nod to that pioneering tour they also included an Australian player, prop Steve Price.

The instigator of that momentous first tour has his own lasting legacy in that Tests between New Zealand and Great Britain are played for the Henry Baskerville Trophy.

— THE WORLD CUP: THE 1970s —

The fourth World Cup tournament took place in Great Britain, and was the first one to be sponsored. As a result, the winners were not presented with the original World Cup but a new one called the V&G Trophy after the sponsors, the Vehicle & General insurance group. Less than impressive, this cup was kept by the winners and never seen again.

Sadly, the magnificent original was stolen from the hotel the Australians were staying in during this tournament. It disappeared for 25 years until it was discovered on a Bradford rubbish tip. Restored to its former glory, it was presented to the winners of the 2000 World Cup.

Great Britain were favourites for the 1970 competition

and topped the table unbeaten. Their opponents in the final, Australia, had only won once but in a niggly final at Headingley, the Kangaroos triumphed 12–7. It was a brutal contest. British centre Syd Hynes and Australian scrum half Billy Smith were sent off and a crucial try was scored by Australian centre John Cootes who was a Catholic priest!

Great Britain gained their revenge two years later in France. They played Australia in the final in Lyon but after extra-time the teams were still locked at 10–10. Clive Sullivan, the British skipper lifted the trophy after his side had been declared winners because they had topped the table with six points to Australia's four. This was to be Britain's last triumph in the competition.

The next World Cup was in 1975 and the format, which had served the competition well since 1954, was abandoned. This tournament was to be held in both hemispheres and spread over nine months with no play-off final, and it was called the World Championship.

With so many Welsh rugby union players having gone north, Wales were able to compete in their own right with England a separate entity. Matches took place in France, England, Wales, Australia and New Zealand, the first one kicking off in March in Toulouse and the last one being held at Salford in November.

Australia topped the table, one point ahead of England, and took the trophy despite not having beaten the English side in their two encounters.

The tournament, however, was a commercial disaster, so not surprisingly the 1977 event had Great Britain once again competing in a four-team competition and, as in 1968, it was staged in both New Zealand and Australia. The Kangaroos topped the table and met second placed Great Britain in the play-off final at the Sydney Cricket Ground, the home side winning 13–12 in a real thriller.

— THE POOR LAD —

The Challenge Cup final at Wembley is one of rugby league's greatest occasions and there was never any doubt that it would return to that historic venue once the new stadium was built in 2007.

Wembley played host to the final from 1929 to 1999 and those matches have produced some of the sport's greatest moments. However, amid all the match-winning performances and wonderful tries there is one final and one incident in that final which make it the most memorable of all.

In 1968 Yorkshire rivals Leeds and Wakefield met in what should have been a classic final, but torrential rain had reduced the pitch to a soggy mess. The match should never have been played but with live television coverage on the BBC and thousands of fans making the trip down to London the game was allowed to go on. It became known as the 'watersplash' final as players floundered and continually lost their footing on the slippery surface.

During the game the heavens opened up again and at one point rained down hailstones. Despite the farcical conditions the game was strangely compelling and the two teams did their best to play rugby. With two minutes remaining the Leeds full back Bev Risman landed his fourth goal, which seemed to seal the contest. However, from the re-start Leeds weren't able to secure the ball and Wakefield wing Ken Hirst, who had already scored one try by dribbling the ball over the wet turf, managed to nip in and boot the ball towards the line.

He raced after it and as defenders struggled to keep their feet, he slid over for a try behind the posts to present the Wakefield goal kicker, Don Fox, with what seemed an easy conversion to win the match. Fox, who had already been chosen as the Man of the Match, had already landed two goals and as he stepped up for the final act of the game many of the Leeds players behind the line simply could not bear to watch.

However, to the amazement of those watching, Fox was unable to secure his footing on the wet turf and sliced his kick wide. As he sank down onto the pitch, completely distraught, TV commentator Eddie Waring summed up the situation perfectly: "He's a poor lad!"

Fox, whose brothers Neil and Peter, both played the game with distinction, said years later. "I won the Lance Todd Trophy that day but nobody ever mentions that. They only remember that old lad who missed that goal."

— RUGBY LEAGUE IN AUSTRALIA —

The visit by the All Golds touring party to Australia in 1907 (see *the All Golds*, page 69) was the catalyst for rugby league to establish itself in that country. As in the north of England, rugby union in Sydney and Brisbane was a predominantly working-class sport.

But the refusal by the authorities to countenance any payment to rugby players, despite huge crowds generating substantial amounts of money, led to the setting up of the New South Wales Rugby League, based in Sydney, and the Queensland Rugby League, based in Brisbane. Crucially the greatest player of the time, Dally Messenger, who joined the All Golds on their tour of Great Britain, had agreed to join the fledgling organisation when he got back.

The new competitions kicked off in 1908 with Easts, Souths, Balmain, Wests, Newtown, Newcastle, Norths, Glebe and Cumberland in the elite NSWRL league. At the end of that first season the first Australian tour to Great Britain took place and adopted the nickname 'the Kangaroos' to distinguish themselves from their union counterparts 'the Wallabies'.

Both toured Britain at the same time, but when the Australian Rugby Union further reduced the players' tour allowances more than half of them switched to rugby league on their return, further boosting the new sport.

In 1909 the first ever Great Britain tour took place with matches in New South Wales, Queensland and New Zealand. Once again this was a huge boost to rugby league and swelled the coffers of the sport, enabling clubs to establish themselves on a secure financial footing.

It was a hold they were never to lose in those states, where rugby league became the number one winter sport. In 1998 the National Rugby League was set up which included teams from Sydney, Brisbane, Melbourne and New Zealand.

— RUGBY LEAGUE CHAMPIONSHIP —

While the Challenge Cup has continued virtually unchanged since its inauguration in 1897, there have been various methods of deciding the champion club at the end of a season.

The very first season of the Northern Union, 1895/96, was straightforward with all 22 clubs playing each other home and away. Manningham emerged as the first champions of the Northern Rugby Football League pipping Halifax by a point thanks to a victory on the last day of the season. Separate Lancashire and Yorkshire Senior Competitions, each made up of 11 clubs, ran concurrently and for the next five seasons the single league was abandoned in favour of these county competitions.

However, at the turn of the century a group of the most powerful clubs decided to form their own Super League for the 1901/02 season, 14 clubs making up a new Northern Rugby Football League with Broughton Rangers the first champions. Over the next three seasons a two-division format was in place but by 1905/06 they were back to just one league of 31 clubs. The unwieldy size of the league made it impossible for home and away fixtures between all the teams so the championship was decided on a percentage basis.

The following season a top four play-off with semi-finals and a final was introduced to try and make the system fairer. The percentage aspect was abandoned in 1930 and only used again during the war years and in 1955/56. But the same basic system prevailed until 1964/65, when the Top Four play-off was enlarged to a Top 16 play-off. This lasted until the re-introduction of two divisions for the 1973/74 season with the side finishing top receiving the League Leaders Trophy.

Although this meant that the First Division clubs could now play each other home and away and the team finishing top were crowned champions, the authorities decided to keep a play-off system because it generated interest and money. After a complicated system involving both First and Second Division clubs in that first season, a Premiership was instigated for the 1974/75 season. This involved the 12 First Division clubs and the top four from the Second but the following season it was restricted to play-offs between the top eight First Division clubs

For the 1986/87 season a Second Division Premiership was introduced with the final being held at Old Trafford before the First Division Premiership final.

Wigan dominated the championship in the late 1980s and early 1990s, topping the First Division seven successive seasons from 1989/90. After winning the Centenary Championship, the last one before the introduction of Super League, Wigan got to keep the trophy.

— EDDIE WARING —

Eddie "up 'n' under" Waring

To a generation of British television viewers, Eddie Waring was 'Mr. Rugby League'. During the 1960s and 1970s he graduated from being BBC TV's commentator on the sport to becoming a genuine TV personality whose fame spread way beyond rugby league.

Some of his catchphrases and quotations have become legendary but his reputation among rugby league fans is somewhat mixed, many feeling that he trivialised the game with his caricature northern image and jokey commentary.

Edward Marsden Waring was born on 21st February 1910 in Dewsbury, Yorkshire. A pupil of Eastborough School, and later Wheelwright Grammar School, he played both codes of rugby and was a good enough footballer to be offered a trial with Nottingham Forest.

Eddie started out as a sports reporter on the *Dewsbury District News* but it was as the youngest manager in the rugby league at his hometown club during the war that he began to make his mark in the game. The young Waring proved a very shrewd operator, taking advantage of a special ruling which allowed clubs to field guest players. He signed a whole host of top performers who were stationed in an army camp about a mile from the Dewsbury ground, which enabled them to win the Challenge Cup in 1943.

In 1946 he paid his own passage on the aircraft carrier *HMS Indomitable* to cover the first post-war Great Britain tour to Australia, the only British journalist to do so. He championed the game as a journalist with the *Sunday Mirror* and a long forgotten publication called *Rugby League Review* and was one of the few reporters to regularly cover the tours.

Legend has it that on the way back from that first trip to Australia, he stopped off in Hollywood, and met Bob Hope who told him that television was the coming medium. Not surprisingly he was the commentator for the first ever televised game of rugby league, the 1948 Challenge Cup final between Bradford Northern and Leeds. Bizarrely, it was shown only to a restricted audience in Birmingham.

The BBC began televising the sport in 1951, kicking off with Great Britain versus New Zealand at Swinton, and Eddie was at the microphone, a job he did for the next 30 years. He became part of the early *Grandstand* team that included David Coleman and six million viewers would tune in on Saturday afternoons to hear Eddie's distinctive, if slightly mangled, Yorkshire tones describe the action with such memorable phrases as "up and under" to describe a high spiraling kick and "early bath" to denote a sending off.

His most memorable quotes include, "I don't know whether that's the ball or his head. We'll know if it stands up".

But his most famous utterance occurred at the end of the 1968 Challenge Cup final between Wakefield Trinity and Leeds. Don Fox missed a last minute conversion, which would have won the cup for Wakefield, and Eddie said of the distraught Fox, "He's a poor lad". It was included in the list of 25 favourite sporting quotes published by *The Times* newspaper in 2006.

When impressionist Mike Yarwood, complete with sheepskin coat and trilby hat, began to do impressions of Waring on his hugely popular television show the rugby league commentator's iconic status was confirmed. Some students even formed the *Eddie Waring Appreciation Society*.

When a new BBC show, *It's a Knockout*, was looking for someone to act as a referee, Eddie was recruited and later became one of the show's presenters alongside Stuart Hall. But it only served to further irritate diehard rugby league supporters who sent a petition to the BBC to complain. The campaign had no effect.

He appeared among a host of stars on the *Morecambe and Wise Christmas Show* in 1977 and also in the comedy programme *The Goodies* alongside Bill Oddie.

His last game for the BBC was the 1981 Premiership final between Hull and Hull Kingston Rovers. He retired aged 71 and died five years later. Love him or loathe him, his name will forever be synonymous with rugby league.

— SUPER LEAGUE RECORDS: PART TWO —

Most tries in a career: 149 by Keith Senior (Leeds Rhinos, Sheffield Eagles, 1996–2006)

Keith Senior scored tries in each of the first four rounds of the inaugural Super League season in 1996 and has been running them in ever since. He notched 40 in four seasons at Sheffield Eagles and added 109 after moving to Leeds. The centre's most prolific season was 2005 when he scored 24 in 23 matches.

Most goals in a career: 979 (including 14 drop goals) by Andrew Farrell (Wigan Warriors, 1996–2004)

Andrew Farrell never finished outside the goal kicking chart's top four in the first six seasons of Super League, heading the list three times. The Wigan Warriors captain's best season total was 164 in 2001. His career record 979 goals include 14 drop goals.

Most points in a career: 2,228 (965 goals, 14 drop goals, 71 tries) by Andrew Farrell (Wigan Warriors,1996–2004)

Even two years after departing to rugby union, Andrew Farrell's record 2,228 points still put him 571 ahead of his nearest challenger, Paul Deacon of the Bradford Bulls. Farrell is the only forward to head the Super League season's points chart – and he has done it twice.

Most appearances in a career (Maximum 293 rounds): 274 (3) by Keith Senior (Leeds Rhinos, 182 (1), Sheffield Eagles 92 (2), 1996–2006) Substitute appearances included in total

Senior missed just 19 Super League matches in his spells with the Rhinos and the Eagles.

Most successive appearances: 143 (three as sub) by Francis Cummins (Leeds Rhinos)

Cummins played in the last round of 1998 and then became the only player to appear in every round over five seasons.

Note: Stats correct up to and including season 2006. These records do not include play-off matches.

— RUGBY À TREIZE —

The introduction of the Catalans Dragons into Super League in 2006 was of huge significance for rugby league in France. It represented a massive step for the game in that country after over 70 years of controversy and turmoil including one of the most shameful acts ever witnessed in sport.

The French had been excluded from rugby union's Five Nations Championship in 1931 over allegations of professionalism and dirty play, a ban which was to last until 1947.

On 31st December 1933 the first ever game of rugby league on French soil took place in Paris at the Stade Pershing when England played Australia. Jean Galia, a French rugby union international, liked what he saw and agreed to put a team together for a six match tour of England in March 1934.

On 13th April, 20,000 turned out to watch France play England at the Stade Buffalo Velodrome. Although the French lost 32–21 it proved the launch pad for a league competition, which blossomed, particularly in the south. By 1939 the national team were strong enough to beat both England and Wales to claim the European crown.

However, the outbreak of war was to prove disastrous for the game. Under the right-wing Vichy government of Marshal Petain, professional sport was banned, although only rugby league felt the full force of the new legislation. The fact that even amateur rugby league was banned led to a long-held belief that the rugby union authorities had used their influence to kill off the sport. Mike Rylance, in his excellent book on the subject, *The Forbidden Game*, explored this issue in an interview with Jean Borotra, a former Wimbledon champion who was appointed by the Vichy government to run a department known as the Commissariat General à L'Education Generale et Sportive, a section of the Ministry of Family and Youth.

Borotra told Rylance: "The banning of rugby league was decided, in 1941, by the director of sports, who was a union player, and who was convinced that the disappearance of rugby league would favour the development of rugby."

Rugby à Treize, as it was known, never recovered and after the war continued to be the very poor relation of rugby union – so much so that even before union went open in 1995, they could not afford to hang onto their best players in the face of the financial inducements of clubs from the supposedly amateur code.

Although France were able to pull off the odd win at international level, when rugby league in Britain and Australia introduced fully professional competitions they simply couldn't compete. Incredibly, rugby league clubs in the south managed to survive although the ill-judged decision to include a Paris-based club in the original Super League, which folded after two seasons, didn't help their cause. As in the north of England, rugby league thrives on support from the community and a strong local identity. The Paris side had neither, they were not in rugby's heartland, were dominated by overseas players and the infrastructure was non-existent.

However, French players appeared in Super League for other clubs and the Rugby Football League began to admit French clubs into the Challenge Cup with Toulouse reaching the semi-finals in 2005. In the following year the Catalan Dragons were admitted to Super League. Based in Perpignan in the heart of rugby country in the south, their entry into Super League had been carefully planned over a number of years. In 2000, two local clubs, XIII Catalan and St Esteve, merged to form Union Treiziste Catalane (UTC), no small achievement given that locals compared it to Wigan joining with St Helens. Unlike the Paris venture, the emphasis was on using a majority of homegrown players and fostering a strong local identity.

Other French clubs have already expressed an interest in joining Super League and ultimately this should lead to a stronger national side.

The main domestic knock-out competition for clubs is the Lord Derby Cup, originally presented by Edward Stanley, the 17th Earl of Derby in 1935.

— THE BIGGEST CROWD —

The biggest crowd ever to attend a rugby league match in Britain was at Bradford's Odsal stadium in 1954 when Halifax met Warrington in a Challenge Cup final replay.

A crowd of 81,777 had watched the two teams play out the first ever Challenge Cup final draw at Wembley on Saturday 24th April and few expected a bigger turn-out than that on the following Wednesday. The Wembley game had been a drab 4–4 affair, the only points coming from penalties; besides, Laurel and Hardy were playing at the Alhambra theatre in the city on the same night!

The kick-off for the replay was scheduled for 7pm and shuttle buses were put on from the town centre, starting at 4:25pm. At the same time 20 trains that had been specially laid on from Warrington were turning up at the nearby Low Moor railway station carrying an estimated 12,000 passengers.

There were 100 gatemen and 150 policemen on duty at Odsal that evening, more than enough for the expected crowd of 70,000. The gates opened at 5pm by which time some people had already been queuing an hour and a half. An hour before kick-off there were already an estimated 60,000 in the ground.

It is said that the traffic jams stretched all the way back to Lancashire as people began pouring into Bradford. These would mainly have been coaches as few people had cars in those days. The official attendance was 102,569 although many believe that the true figure was nearer 120,000 because many fences had been flattened and in all the photographs of the event spectators are crowded around the pitch. Incredibly there were no major casualties, merely the usual reports of people fainting.

Warrington won the match 8–4 with tries from Jim Challinor and Gerry Helme with Harry Bath adding a goal. Halifax's only points came from two penalties from Tuss Griffiths.

Remarkably just over an hour after the final whistle, the crowd had reportedly been fully dispersed from Odsal. Today the capacity at Odsal is 25,000 and Bradford, now called the Bulls, after toying with the idea of relocating, have an ambitious plan to redevelop the site.

The attendance remained a world record for one game between two clubs but in 1999, 107,558 crammed into Stadium Australia for the 1999 NRL Grand Final between Melbourne Storm and the St George Illawara Dragons, with Melbourne winning 20–18.

— RUGBY LEAGUE LEGENDS: BRIAN BEVAN —

Warrington try machine Brian Bevan

Brian Bevan was the greatest try scorer in the history of rugby league. Yet the Australian, who never represented his country, was the most unlikely looking rugby player you'll ever come across.

Skinny, balding, swathed in bandages with cheeks puffed out, he looked like an OAP running for a bus rather than a lethal winger going for the try line. But in an astonishing 19 year career he amassed an incredible 796 tries, over 100 more than his nearest rival, Billy Boston, a record which is unlikely to be beaten.

Although Australian born, Bevan is almost forgotten in his homeland but in Warrington, where he spent most of his career, he is a revered figure. When the club relocated to their new ground they took the Brian Bevan memorial statue, which had been erected on a roundabout just outside Wilderspool, with them and it has a special place outside the Halliwell Jones stadium.

Bevan was born in 1924 in the Bondi area of Sydney. His father had played for the Eastern Suburbs and the young Brian joined them as well but played just eight games for them without scoring a try. When war broke out he became a naval stoker and came to Britain aboard HMAS Australia in 1945.

He had a letter of introduction to Bill Shankland, a fellow Australian who had played for Easts and the 1929/30 Kangaroos and latterly for Warrington. Shankland advised him to try his luck with Leeds, then Hunslet, both of whom took one look at the strange looking 21-year-old and declined to sign him. Bevan turned up at Warrington who gave him an anonymous 'A' team trial that November. He scored a try, played in the first team the following week and was signed for £300. But he had to return to Australia to get demobbed before coming back to embark upon his extraordinary career.

In his first season at Wilderspool, 1946/47, Bevan topped the try-scoring list with 48. Within four years he had overtaken the club try-scoring record of 215 that had taken Jack Fish 13 seasons to reach at the turn of the century. Bevan topped the British try-scoring table five times in 15 seasons, his greatest year being 1952/53 when he scored 72, just eight short of the record held by Albert Rosenfeld of Huddersfield. A hundred times he scored at least a hat-trick of tries in a match and twice he notched up seven for Warrington.

Speed was Bevan's biggest asset. He took part in many professional sprint meetings and rarely lost, but to be a successful rugby winger you need a lot more. He had great anticipation, could swerve and step and had an instinct for being in the right place at the right time

Although he never represented Australia he did get a taste of international football by playing for the Other Nationalities, a team of self-imposed exiles, 26 times. During his 16 years with Warrington, he won two Challenge Cups, three championships, a Lancashire Cup and six Lancashire League titles. He played his last game for them on Easter Monday 1962 but in semi-retirement he turned out for Blackpool Borough for a couple of years and died just down the coast at Southport in 1991.

He was inducted into the British Rugby League Hall of Fame in 1998 and seven years later his exploits were finally recognised in his home country when the Australian Rugby League admitted him to their Hall of Fame.

Brian Eyrl Bevan
Born: 24th June 1924, Sydney, Australia
Position: Wing
Playing career: 1942–64
Clubs: Warrington, Blackpool Borough
Scoring: 796 tries

— MOST TRIES —

George 'Tich' West was a little winger who made a big try-scoring impact in just one match – as the scorer of a record 11 touchdowns. The feat has defied a succession of legendary try-scorers for almost a century. Yet West never gained international honours and notched up an unremarkable 98 tries in 217 appearances for Hull Kingston Rovers.

Here's the list of the top individual try-scoring feats in a single match:

Year	Tries	Player	Opponents
1905	11	George West (Hull Kingston R.)	Brookland Rovers*
1951	10	Lionel Cooper (Huddersfield)	Keighley
1992	10	Martin Offiah (Wigan)	Leeds
1992	10	Shaun Edwards (Wigan)	Swinton
1935	9	Ray Markham (Huddersfield)	Featherstone Rovers
1994	9	Greg Austin (Huddersfield)	Blackpool Gladiators*
1907	8	Dai Thomas (Dewsbury)	Liverpool City
1911	8	Albert Rosenfeld (Huddersfield)	Wakefield Trinity
1913	8	Fred Webster (Leeds)	Coventry
1931	8	Eric Harris (Leeds)	Bradford Northern
1948	8	Lionel Cooper (Huddersfield)	Yorkshire Amateurs*
1957	8	Keith Williams (Halifax)	Dewsbury

* Amateurs

Great Britain on tour

Year	Tries	Scorer	Opponents
1946	17	Ernest Ward	Mackay (Australia)
1914	15	Alf Wood	South Australia
1950	15	Jim Ledgard	Wide Bay (Australia)
1954	15	Lewis Jones	Southern New South Wales
1958	15	Eric Fraser	North Queensland (Australia)

England under-21s

Year	Tries	Scorer	Opponents
2001	18	Rob Burrows	South Africa

— COUNTY CUPS —

The Lancashire and Yorkshire Cups were introduced in the 1905/06 season for the professional clubs of the counties, although Lancashire included the Cumbrian clubs and Fulham when they came into being. Both cups had a knock-out format and were played in the early part of the season. The cups produced some memorable matches but both competitions ceased in 1993.

The Lancashire and Yorkshire League competitions continued to run after the formation of the Northern Rugby Football League in 1901/02 with fixtures against clubs in their counties counting towards a league table. For one season, 1962/63, they were replaced by the Western Division and Eastern Division Championships respectively with each team playing eight fixtures culminating in a top four play-off.

The county leagues were eventually laid to rest in 1970.

— THE CHALLENGE CUP:
THE WEMBLEY YEARS, PART TWO —

The 50th final at Wembley in 1985 between Wigan and Hull proved to be one of the best. Hull trailed 22–8 early in the second half but their Australian international scrum half Peter Sterling led a dramatic fight back. They equalled Wigan's five tries but couldn't kick their goals and ended up losing 28–24.

The 1987 match between Halifax and St Helens produced the first receipts of £1 million and the following year began an unprecedented domination by one club – Wigan. As the first team to be fully professional and with the money to recruit the best players from home and abroad they dominated rugby league in the late 1980s and early 1990s, winning the Challenge Cup for eight consecutive years.

Their 1994 26–16 win over Leeds saw a try by Wigan wing Martin Offiah, which many consider the greatest try ever scored at the old stadium (see *Rugby League Legends: Martin Offiah*, page 7).

The first final of the Super League era in 1996 between the Bradford Bulls and St Helens saw the greatest comeback ever seen at the Twin Towers. Thirteen minutes into the second half Bradford looked to have built an unassailable 26–12 lead. However, the St Helens scrum half Bobbie Goulding began bombarding the Bulls' full back Nathan Graham with high kicks. Graham spilled three in seven minutes, all of which led to tries, turning the game on its head. Despite the first ever hat-trick at Wembley by Bradford's Robbie Paul, the Bulls lost 40–32.

The 1998 final between the Sheffield Eagles and Wigan looked such a foregone conclusion that only 60,669 supporters turned up to watch it – the lowest crowd since 1946. However, those that made the effort saw the biggest upset in the history of Challenge Cup finals. Sheffield, who had only been in existence for 14 years, were taking on the biggest name in the game who had won more finals than anyone. But Sheffield coach John Kear had done his homework and his side carried out their game plan to perfection running out 17–8 winners.

The final Challenge Cup final at the old stadium took place in 1999 when the Leeds Rhinos beat the London Broncos with Leeds winger Leroy Rivett scoring a record four tries.

For the next eight years the Challenge Cup final went on the road being played at Murrayfield, Twickenham and the Millennium Stadium before returning to the new Wembley in 2007 with St Helen's beating Catalans Dragons 30–8.

— THE LONGEST TRY —

There have been plenty of length-of-the-field touchdowns in rugby league by some of the game's greatest names, but the credit for the longest try goes to a little known winger from a now defunct club.

On 21st February 1982 Joe Bardgett, playing on the left wing for Carlisle during a Second Division match at Brunton Park against Halifax, ran an incredible 139 yards (127 metres) to touchdown.

Bardgett fielded a kick by the touchline near his own try line and then ran back into the in-goal area before emerging between the posts. He burst down the middle through a knot of Halifax defenders and ended up putting the ball down between the posts at the other end. A Carlisle official measured the distance after the match, which the home side won 20–0.

— MOST GOALS IN A MATCH —

The great Jim Sullivan missed with only two conversion attempts when he landed his record 22 goals in Wigan's 116–0 St Valentine's Day massacre of Flimby and Fothergill amateurs in a Challenge Cup-tie in 1925. It was a consistency that continued throughout his career. He kicked a century of goals in 18 successive seasons after leaving Welsh rugby union in 1921.

Year	Goals	Player	Opponents
1925	22	Jim Sullivan (Wigan)	Flimby & Fothergill*
1914	18	Major Holland (Huddersfield)	Swinton Park*
2005	18	Lee Birdseye (Rochdale Hornets)	Illingworth*
1973	17	Geoff 'Sammy' Lloyd (Castleford)	Millom*
1994	17	Darren Carter (Barrow)	Nottingham City*
2001	17	Iestyn Harris (Leeds Rhinos)	Swinton Lions
1986	16	Paul Loughlin (St Helens)	Carlisle
1976	15	Mick Stacey (Leigh)	Doncaster
1992	15	John Wasyliw (Keighley Cougars)	Nottingham City
2000	15	Martin Wood (Keighley Cougars)	Lancashire Lynx
2000	15	Andrew Farrell (Wigan Warriors)	Whitehaven Warriors

— LONDON CALLING: PART TWO —

After the failures of Acton & Willesden and Streatham & Mitcham in the 1930s, that appeared to be that for rugby league in London. That was until June 1980 when Ernie Clay, chairman of Fulham Football Club, announced the formation of a rugby league team to play at Craven Cottage. The venture was seen as a way of generating extra income, and although the Rugby Football League accepted the new club into the Second Division of the competition it was considered something of a hair-brained scheme.

However, Fulham hired Widnes scrum half Reg Bowden as player/coach and recruited wisely. The opening match at Craven Cottage in September 1980 was a momentous day for the sport as nearly 10,000 fans watched the new team beat Wigan, who had been relegated from the First Division the previous season, 24–5.

That first season Fulham rode the crest of a wave, beating Leeds in the John Player trophy in front of 12,583 and getting the biggest ever crowd for a London rugby league club when 15,013 turned up to see them take on Wakefield in the Challenge Cup. The club won promotion in that first season but struggled with their small squad at the higher level and were relegated.

At the end of the fourth season, continuing financial losses saw the plug pulled at Craven Cottage, but thanks to the backing of supporters Roy and Barbara Close the club survived, although they led a nomadic existence playing at many grounds including Crystal Palace, Chiswick Polytechnic and Barnet Copthall.

In 1991 the club's name was changed to the London Crusaders and during a period of improving fortunes they made the 1994 Divisional Premiership final at Old Trafford. A new dawn arrived when the Brisbane Broncos bought the club and changed the name to the London Broncos.

With the advent of Super League in 1996, the Broncos moved to south east London to play at the Valley, home of

Charlton Athletic FC. But after one season they were on their way back to west London to play at the Stoop Memorial Ground. The Virgin Group then became the majority shareholder and in 1997 it finally looked as though they had achieved the breakthrough, finishing second in Super League and attracting good crowds for their wins over Bradford and Wigan plus. Their victory over the Canberra Raiders in the World Club Challenge was a high point.

In 1999, the Broncos reached the Challenge Cup final in what proved to be the last rugby league game ever to be played at the old Wembley Stadium, losing to the Leeds Rhinos. But they were off on their travels again for another season at the Valley with supporter David Hughes purchasing the majority shareholding from Virgin in a major restructuring of the club.

The Broncos moved back to West London in 2002 to play at Brentford's Griffin Park. Another crisis loomed in early 2005 when the other Super League clubs only just agreed to allow them to continue after a financial re-structuring. Months later the Broncos became Harlequins RL under new chairman Ian Lenagan and moved to their new home at the Twickenham Stoop.

Away from the elite level, rugby league has made enormous strides in London and the south-east. A summer conference competition was launched in the late 1990s which has spread the game to all parts of the country. The London Skolars, founded in 1995 and based in North London, became one of the founding members of the Southern Conference in 1997, the forerunner to the Summer Conference. Later that year, they entered the BARLA National Conference League, as the only club south of Sheffield. In 2003 the London Skolars became the first club in 80 years to make the jump from the amateur ranks to the professional leagues.

In addition, there are amateur clubs all over London and the south-east and the number of schools now playing rugby league has rocketed. London rugby league has come a long way from the dog tracks of Acton and Streatham.

— THE WORLD CUP: THE 1980S —

After five tournaments in nine years between 1968–77 everything went quiet on the World Cup front with tours taking precedent. However, when the competition did reappear in the mid-1980s the game's administrators came up with a bizarre concept.

The tournament was to be spread over three years, starting in 1985, with one Test in a series between the participants designated a World Cup game. Points would be awarded and a table would then be made up. There was some logic to this because, in some cases, it would give a meaningless final game in a three Test series some interest. A fifth nation, Papua New Guinea, was added to the longstanding quartet, but the drawn out nature of the contest had some farcical consequences.

The first game between New Zealand and Australia in Auckland was repeated three years later in the final. In the intervening years, not only had players and coaches changed but also the very nature of the game. The French were unable to fulfil their fixtures in the southern hemisphere due to financial constraints so their opponents were automatically awarded two points.

The Kiwis won the opening encounter of the tournament 18–0 but were beaten 25–12 in the final three years later in 1988. The one positive note was a crowd of over 47,000, which proved there was an appetite for league in New Zealand and this ultimately led to the creation of the Auckland Warriors.

Remarkably, the next tournament was run along the same lines as the last one, a three-year affair beginning in 1989 and culminating in a final in 1992. At least all five competing nations managed to complete their fixtures this time with Australia topping the table unbeaten and Great Britain and New Zealand finishing joint second with 10 points. The British qualified for the final thanks to a better points for and against aggregate and with the Australians happy to give up home advantage, the match was set for October 1992 at Wembley.

A huge crowd of 73,631 turned out and in a tense, closely fought final the Kangaroos edged it 10–6 to retain the trophy.

— APPEARANCES IN A CAREER —

They say records are made to be broken, but Jim Sullivan's incredible 928 appearances will last for all time. The Wigan full back's 25-year career spanned an era when clubs played up to 50 matches a season compared with today's 35 or so. Sullivan's total was also boosted by 53 matches on three Great Britain tours of Australia and New Zealand.

Here's the list of the top 10 players with the highest number of total career appearances:

Apps	Player	Clubs	Career
928	Jim Sullivan	Wigan + (wartime) guest Dewsbury, Keighley, Bradford N.	1921–46
873	Gus Risman	Salford, Workington T., Batley	1929–54
828 (28)	Neil Fox	Wakefield Tr., Bradford N., Hull KR., York, Bramley, Huddersfield	1956–79
776 (57)	Jeff Grayshon	Dewsbury, Bradford N., Leeds, Featherstone R., Batley	1969–95
740 (46)	Graham Idle	Bramley, Wakefield Trinity, Bradford N., Hunslet, Rochdale Hornets, Sheffield E., Doncaster, Nottingham, Highfield	1969–93
738 (25)	Colin Dixon	Halifax, Salford, Hull KR	1961–81
727 (9)	Paul Charlton	Workington T., Salford, Blackpool B.	1961–81

695 (26)	Keith Mumby	Bradford N., Sheffield Eagles, Keighley Cougars, Ryedale-York, Wakefield T.	1973–95
691 (1)	Ernie Ashcroft	Wigan, Huddersfield, Warrington	1942–62
688	Brian Bevan	Warrington, Blackpool	1945–64

Note: Figures in brackets denote substitute appearances included in main total.

— OLD DIVISION ONE RECORDS —

Most tries in a match by a player: 6, by Shane Cooper (St. Helens) v Hull, 17th February 1988

Most tries in a season by a player: 44, by Ellery Hanley (Wigan) 1986/87

Widest winning margin: Leeds 90 Barrow 0, 11th February 1990

Scoreless draw: Wigan 0 Castleford 0, 26th January 1974

Highest score draw: Leeds 46 Sheffield Eagles 46, 10th April 1994

Longest winning run: 25, by St Helens. Won last 13 of 1985/86 and first 12 of 1986/87 (Also longest unbeaten run)

Longest losing run from start of season: 20, by Whitehaven 1983/84

Longest opening run without a win: 23, including three draws, by Whitehaven 1981/82

Biggest attendance: 29,839 Wigan v St Helens, 9th April 1993

Note: These records have not been beaten in the Super League era and take into account matches played in the old style Division One which ran from 1973/74 to 1994/95 inclusive, and the 1995/96 Centenary Championship

— MASCOT MAYHEM —

The advent of Super League and the new razzamatazz surrounding it proved a growth industry for club mascots. While some clubs had dabbled with them – who could forget a man dressed as a pie walking round Wigan's old Central Park ground? – summer rugby became something of a boom time for all manner and means of silly costumes and papier-mâché heads.

One of the most famous mascots is Ronnie the Rhino, whose antics on the Headingley turf enthral kids and a few adults as well. He stood for Parliament in the summer of that year and polled 47 votes, garnering international as well as national media coverage. His biggest rival is Bradford's Bullman, who now has a son, Bullboy. Castleford also have an extended family with Tigerman and Tigertot.

St Helens have a man dressed up as a St Bernard dog. He, or rather his head, became the focus of attention after Saints' last gasp wonder try in the dying seconds to win a play-off match against Bradford at Knowsley Road in 2000. Scrum half Sean Long was so overcome with emotion he grabbed the head off the mascot and ran back onto the pitch wearing it. He was only persuaded to take it off when it was pointed out that he had to take the conversion!

Billy and Bluey of the Halifax Blue Sox get the vote for the daftest pair of mascots. Quite what these two gormless-looking creatures dressed in blue and white did for the marketing of the club is anybody's guess. Thankfully they are no more and the club is just plain old Halifax again

Gateshead Thunder may have only lasted one season in Super League but they boasted the most charismatic mascot in Captain Thunder – a masked vision in purple Lycra. There's more than a passing reference to the greatly missed Thunder in Salford's latest incarnation Ignito, a bloke in a tight red Lycra suit, with a helmet and dark visor who runs out before home games with a red flare.

— EIGHTIES EXPANSION —

The introduction of Fulham in 1980 sparked a rash of new teams springing up outside the rugby league heartland, but few survived.

Carlisle City had originally joined the rugby league in 1928/29 but only lasted ten matches. Their new venture began in 1981 and initially the team weren't much better, being walloped 112–0 by St Helens in 1986. However, they hung around for another decade, merging with Barrow at the end of the 1997 season to become Barrow Border Raiders in Nation League Two.

In Wales, Cardiff City joined in 1981 and lasted three seasons. The north Midlands saw the Mansfield Marksman kick off the 1984/85 season and they became Nottingham City in 1989/90 before folding. The south saw a second club, Kent Invicta, based at Maidstone. In 1984/85 they became Southend Invicta before calling it a day the following year.

The Scarborough Pirates played just one season in 1991/92, the most memorable thing about them being their colours which were royal purple and gold.

Sheffield Eagles, formed in 1984 by Gary Hetherington were by far the most successful. They caused one of the biggest upsets in Challenge Cup history when they beat Wigan at Wembley in 1998 and played in Super League. They also produced a string of great players including Great Britain internationals Darryl Powell, Keith Senior, Mark Aston, Paul Broadbent, Lee Jackson and Dale Laughton. However, financial pressures forced them to merge with Huddersfield to form the Huddersfield-Sheffield Giants but the Sheffield part soon disappeared. Thanks, though, to the efforts of stalwart Mark Aston, the Sheffield Eagles were resurrected and currently play in the National Leagues.

There have been several attempts to establish a

professional club in the north-east and in 1999 Gateshead Thunder were awarded a Super League franchise with former St Helens coach Shaun McRae as coach. They lasted just one season before 'merging' with Hull Sharks although they effectively disappeared. However, thanks to the enthusiasm of some die-hard fans, a new Gateshead Thunder was constituted and they play in the National Leagues.

— TAKING THE STRINE —

In the 1980s the British game saw an unprecedented influx of Australian and New Zealand coaches into the game. They brought a wealth of talent, skills and technical know-how into the domestic game but they also brought with them a whole new language.

Suddenly, the sport was awash with new words and phrases, which subsequently have become common parlance in today's game. Apart from starting just about every sentence with the word 'mate' even though you may have only just clapped eyes on the bloke, here are some words and phrases to look out for.

The play-the-ball area was pretty self-explanatory, but Australians decided to call it a 'ruck'. To most rugby followers in this country a 'ruck' is essentially a rugby union term for what happens when a player gets tackled on the ground and a pile up of bodies ensues as both sides try to 'ruck' the ball out with their feet. It has got precisely nothing to do with the play-the-ball in league but obviously Aussies think differently.

The big tough blokes who do all the hard graft up front were always called 'forwards' and collectively known as 'the pack'. But our antipodean friends decided to join the two together so now they talk about 'the forward pack' using the word 'forward' as an adjective. To distinguish it from the 'backward pack' or the 'sideways pack', possibly!

Even more bizarrely, the Aussie influx has seen dressing rooms become 'sheds' which to most people in this country are places for storing gardening tools and old bikes. Similarly, a pass out of a tackle has become an 'offload' and stealing the ball out of a tackle is now known as 'reefing'.

And what about the word 'ordinary'? To most people this would mean acceptable, okay, or fine. But if an Aussie coach describes a tackle or a kick as 'ordinary', he actually means it's pretty poor. And the word 'dirty' takes on a whole new meaning in Aussie parlance. If a player says that the coach was pretty 'dirty' or 'filthy' it doesn't mean that he hasn't had a bath, but that he was critical or not very happy.

'A rake' in the English language tends to mean a garden implement or a bounder from a Victorian novel, but to our antipodean cousins it's their word for a hooker. Similarly a 'stanza' is something you get in a poem but to them it means 'half', as in first half and second half.

Just as confusingly, a drop goal has become a 'field goal' and if you go to Australia don't go asking about the rugby match or they'll direct you to the nearest union game. No, rugby league over there is 'footie'.

Sky's Dewsbury-born rugby league commentator Mike Stephenson, who has spent time playing and living in Australia, has popularised many of these new words, although there are suspicions that terms like 'power play' to describe a team who pass the ball on the sixth tackle instead of kicking it and 'red zone' to describe the area 20 metres in front of the try line may well be his own creations.

And finally guys, we know Salford sounds like it should be pronounced 'Sal-ford' but it's actually 'Sol–ford'!

— RUGBY LEAGUE LEGENDS: ELLERY HANLEY —

Ellery Hanley: a modern rugby league great

Ellery Hanley was the greatest player of his generation. He made an impact on both the domestic scene and in Australia where they nicknamed him 'The Black Pearl'. Hanley not only played for Great Britain with distinction but also became the first black coach of any British national sporting team.

Hanley was the prototype modern rugby league player, strong, athletic with a thorough understanding of the game and a steely determination to succeed. Born in Leeds, he was spotted playing amateur rugby league for local side Corpus Christi and signed by Bradford in 1978 as a centre. In 1984 he made his debut for Great Britain and began his inexorable rise to the pinnacle of the game.

He was one of the stars of the 1984 Lions tour to Australia and in the 1984/85 season he became the first player since Billy Boston in 1962 to score more than 50 tries in a season. Shortly after he was transferred to Wigan in a world record £150,000 deal.

In his second season at Central Park he scored 63 tries playing at centre, stand off and loose forward, an all-time record for a non-winger. In February 1987 he made the permanent move to loose forward and became an integral part of the all-conquering Wigan side of the late 1980s and early 1990s. In 1987 he was appointed Great Britain captain and on the 1988 tour down under took the Lions the closest they had been for a decade to regaining the Ashes.

While on tour he was signed by Balmain on a short-term contract and was instrumental in taking them to the 1988 Australian Grand Final. Championship, Challenge Cup, Lancashire Cup and Regal Trophy winners' medals continued to flow but in 1991 he was involved in another world record transfer deal when he moved from Wigan to Leeds for £250,000. Despite being over 30, he still managed to score 100 tries for Leeds and in 1995, at the age of 34, he broke the record for most tries in a season by a forward with a tally of 41.

As a coach he was also successful, coaching Great Britain in the 1994 Ashes series and guiding St Helens to a Super League triumph in 1999. Awarded the MBE in 1990, he was inducted into the Hall of Fame in 2005.

Ellery Hanley
Born: 27th March 1961, Leeds
Position: Centre, stand off, loose forward
Playing career: 1978–95
Clubs: Bradford Northern, Wigan, Leeds, Balmain (Aus), Western Suburbs (Aus)
International record: Great Britain (35(1) apps, 20 tries), England (2 apps, 2 tries)
Scoring: 428 tries, 94 goals, 6 drop goals

— FLOODLIT TROPHY —

The 1960s saw more and more rugby league clubs installing floodlights and with the advent of a second BBC channel, the two came together in the BBC2 Floodlit Trophy which was born in 1965.

Surprisingly, there had been a similar tournament on the fledgling ITV network ten years earlier. Eight clubs participated in a series of games played at football grounds in the London area, with Warrington beating Leigh 43–18 in the final at Loftus Road. Obviously the controller of BBC2, David Attenborough, liked the idea and the competition kicked off with eight clubs but by the time it ended in 1980, 22 were taking part. Apart from the first two seasons it was contested on a knock-out basis.

In 1966 the competition experimented with limited tackles, which was so successful that it became universal. Games were played on Tuesday evenings with one selected for broadcasting.

In 1974 Bramley beat Widnes in the final, the only trophy the Yorkshire club have ever won and it had to be played in the afternoon because of power cuts and the introduction of a three-day week due to a miners' strike.

The BBC eventually scrapped the competition due to financial cuts.

— MAN OF STEEL —

The Rugby Football League instigated its own awards in 1977. Sponsored by Trumanns Steel for the first six years, they have become universally known as the 'Man of Steel' awards. The top award goes to the player judged to have made the biggest impact during the season.

Originally covering all divisions, since the inception of Super League the award solely concerns the elite competition. In addition to the Man of Steel there is also the Players' Player of the Year, Coach of the Year, and

Referee of the Year. The presentations are made at a glittering awards ceremony in Manchester prior to the Grand Final.

Super League's men of steel:

1996 Andy Farrell (Wigan)
1997 James Lowes (Bradford)
1998 Iestyn Harris (Leeds)
1999 Adrian Vowles (Castleford)
2000 Sean Long (St Helens)
2001 Paul Sculthorpe (St Helens)
2002 Paul Sculthorpe (St Helens)
2003 Jamie Peacock (Bradford)
2004 Andrew Farrell (Wigan)
2005 Jamie Lyon (St Helens)
2006 Paul Wellens (St Helens)

— TOP 10 SUPER LEAGUE APPEARANCES —

Apps	Player	Years
274 (3)	Keith Senior (Leeds, Sheffield)	1996–2006
255 (10)	Keiron Cunningham (St Helens)	1996–2006
240 (26)	Robbie Paul (Huddersfield, Bradford)	1996–2006
235 (15)	Michael Wainwright (Warrington, Salford)	1996–2006
231 (23)	Terry Newton (Bradford, Wigan, Leeds)	1996–2006
229 (11)	Lee Briers (Warrington, St Helens)	1997–2006
229 (39)	Terry O'Connor (Widnes, Wigan)	1996–2005
229 (20)	Danny Orr (Wigan, Castleford)	1997–2006
228 (34)	Mick Cassidy (Widnes, Wigan)	1996–2005
226 (75)	Jamie Field (Wakefield, Huddersfield, Leeds)	1996–2006

Note: Stats correct up to and including season 2006. From a possible 293 rounds over 11 seasons. Substitute appearances included in total.

— HAND IT OVER —

In the early years the Challenge Cup was presented to the winning captain by the wives of the presidents of the Northern Union. Later the presentation ceremony branched out to include various officials, local dignitaries and celebrities.

The first royal to hand over the trophy was HRH The Prince of Wales in 1933 while in 1938 Australian cricketer Don Bradman did the honours.

The first prime minister to present the cup was Clement Attlee in 1946. Two years later the reigning monarch King George VI handed over the trophy and the Queen did her first presentation in 1960. Field Marshall Montgomery presented in 1963 and Lord Mountbatten 10 years later.

But the Challenge Cup final is about much more than just the final. There have always been amateur clubs involved in the early rounds – indeed that first competition in 1897 included the likes of Warrington Locos, Leeds Parish Church and Atherton Hornets. More recently, French clubs were admitted with Toulouse becoming the first French team to make the semi-finals in 2006 and the following year the Catalans Dragons reached the final.

The current Challenge Cup is a replica of the original which was presented for the last time in 2001 to St Helens skipper Chris Joynt following his side's 13–6 success over Bradford.

After 100 finals and numerous batterings over the years, Sheffield-based manufacturers John Spencer Goldsmiths were commissioned to make the new trophy, which took 800 man-hours to produce and was presented for the first time at Murrayfield in 2002 to Wigan skipper Kris Radlinski. It is an exact replica of the original, complete with engravings, but has a strengthened neck.

— VETERAN PERFORMERS —

The following players have appeared in at least one match in every season of Super League:

Chris Chester* (Halifax 1996–99; Wigan 1999–01; Hull 2002–06)

Keiron Cunningham* (St Helens 1996–2006)

Jamie Field (Leeds 1996–97; Huddersfield 1998; Wakefield 1999–2006)

Paul Johnson (Wigan 1996–2003; Bradford 2006)

Toa Kohe-Love* (Warrington 1996–2001, 2005–06; Hull 2002–03; Bradford 2004)

Sean Long (Wigan 1996–97; St Helens 1997–2006)

Terry Newton (Leeds 1996–99; Wigan 2000–05; Bradford 2006)

Robbie Paul* (Bradford 1996–2005; Huddersfield 2006)

Kris Radlinski* (Wigan 1996–2006)

Paul Sculthorpe* (Warrington 1996–97; St Helens 1998–2006)

Keith Senior* (Sheffield 1996–99; Leeds 1999–2006)

Marcus St. Hilaire (Leeds 1996–2002; Huddersfield 2003–05; Bradford 2006)

Mike Wainwright* (Warrington 1996–99, 2003–06; Salford 2000–02)

* Played in first ever round

— LET THERE BE LIGHT —

Bradford Northern became the first rugby league club to install floodlights in 1951. The first match took place at Odsal on 31st October against the touring New Zealanders with 29,072 turning up to see Northern win 13–8. Leigh followed in October 1953 when they hosted a Lancashire v Yorkshire match, but it wasn't until the 1960s that the majority of clubs got around to installing floodlights.

— IN UNION WITH LEAGUE —

When the England rugby union team won the World Cup in Australia in 2003 the rugby league influence consisted of more than just try scorer Jason Robinson.

A number of Sir Clive Woodward's coaching team had rugby league entries on their CVs. Phil Larder, who was brought in as a defensive specialist and became assistant coach, played league for Oldham and Whitehaven. He then coached a number of clubs before taking on the England team in the 1995 RL World Cup and was in charge of Great Britain on their 1996 tour of New Zealand. Mike Ford, another former rugby league player, later replaced Larder as defensive coach.

Dave Alred, who is regarded as the world's leading kicking coach, played for Sheffield Eagles in their inaugural season. He was employed by the England rugby union team in 1998 and worked with Jonny Wilkinson among others. Alred was also responsible for the players' mental preparation and became part of the coaching team in the 2003 World Cup.

Joe Lydon had an outstanding career with Widnes, Wigan and Great Britain before taking up a position with the Rugby Football Union. He was appointed coach to the England Sevens and 'A' team and after the World Cup triumph became backs coach to the senior team.

— SUBSTITUTES —

In 1964 substitutes were allowed for the first time but only for injuries and only up to half-time. A year later subs could be introduced for any reason and in 1969 were allowed at any stage of the game. Unlike rugby union, substituted players can go back on in league. These days teams start with four players on the bench and they can make up to 12 interchanges during the game, which includes blood bin replacements.

— THE CENTENARY WORLD CUP, 1995 —

The centenary of the birth of rugby league was the catalyst for the 1995 World Cup tournament played in Great Britain. The competition reverted to a much more traditional format and proved to be one of the most successful ever staged.

Ten countries took part with Great Britain once again split into England and Wales. The South Sea nations of Fiji, Samoa and Tonga joined Papua New Guinea, Australia, France and New Zealand plus emerging nation South Africa.

The teams were divided into three pools, two of three nations and one of four playing matches in England and Wales over three weeks in October. The tournament was blessed with good weather and some terrific matches and got off to a great start when England beat Australia at Wembley.

Some of the most memorable contests involved the South Sea nations while the Welsh team featured many former rugby union greats who had gone north. Due to rugby union going open that year this was to be the last time the Welsh rugby league team would feature so many great names.

England made the final by beating Wales at Old Trafford while Australia needed extra-time to beat New Zealand at Huddersfield. In the final, staged at Wembley, Australia once again rose to the big occasion, beating England 16–8.

Adding to the overall spectacle, an Emerging Nations tournament was run alongside the main competition. The seven countries taking part were the Cook Islands, Ireland, Scotland, Russia, the USA, Moldova and Morocco, with the Cook Islands beating Ireland in the final.

— WORLD CLUB CHALLENGE —

The competition began unofficially in 1976 when English champions St Helens went to Australia to play the Australian champions Eastern Suburbs in Sydney with the home side winning 25–2. It was 11 years until a similar match was staged, this time at Central Park where Wigan took on Manly. It was a bold initiative by the British club as the national side hadn't beaten Australia for over ten years. But on a magical night Wigan beat Manly 8–2 in an enthralling contest. What made victory all the sweeter was that their team was made up entirely of British players.

The first official World Club Challenge was contested between Widnes and Canberra in 1989. Three further matches, each involving Wigan, were staged through the early 1990s. With the outbreak of the Australian Super League War in 1995, the World Club Challenge was suspended. In 1997, to compensate for the disruption caused by the dispute, a World Club Championship was staged with all 12 Northern Hemisphere clubs pitted against the ten from the Southern Hemisphere. No European club made it through to the semi-finals with Brisbane Broncos beating the Hunter Mariners 36–12 in an all-Australian final.

The one-off challenge match was resurrected in 2000, played between the winners of the National Rugby League in Australia and the European Super League. It has been since contested annually in various venues in the United Kingdom and usually staged early in the domestic season or just before its start.

Wigan are the only team to have played the Australian champions in their own back yard. In 1994 they went to Brisbane and beat the Broncos 20–14 at the ANZ Stadium. All other games have taken place in Britain with the home clubs doing particularly well. As a result, many Australians cite ground advantage and the wintry conditions to excuse poor performances by some of their clubs. However, various Super League champions have expressed a desire to play the match in Australia but these requests have fallen on deaf ears.

— RUGBY LEAGUE'S VC —

Bravery and toughness are qualities synonymous with rugby league and no one displayed them to greater effect than John (Jack) Harrison. Born in Hull on 12th November 1890 he became a teacher first in York and then back in his native city.

While teaching in York he came to the attention of the local rugby league club and played for York five times in the 1911/12 season, scoring three tries. He returned to his native Hull and five days after getting married played his first match for Hull FC on 5th September 1912.

In the 1913/14 season he scored a club record 52 tries, going on to score a total of 106 tries in 116 matches for the club up to 1916, one of which earned them a Challenge Cup final victory over Wakefield Trinity. Jack was selected to tour Australia in 1914, but it was cancelled due to the outbreak of the First World War so he enlisted in the army.

On completion of his officer training he was posted to 6 Platoon of the 11th Battalion East Yorkshire Regiment as a (temporary) 2nd Lieutenant. The brigade was stationed on the western front in the Somme area where an average of 300 men were being killed every day. In February 1917 the Hull brigade entered the front line.

On 3rd May the brigade were sent to attack the German lines at Oppy Wood, a well-defended area considered a vital target for the British advance. Jack's platoon were pinned down by heavy machine gun fire, so, armed with only a pistol and hand grenades, he set about eliminating the enemy position.

Using his rugby skills, he dodged between shell holes and weaved in and out of the barbed wire as he advanced towards the enemy machine gun posts. While tossing a grenade in the direction of the machine gun post he was hit. The gun fell silent and Jack was never seen again.

King George V presented Jack's wife Lillian with a Victoria Cross at Buckingham Palace in March 1918. A fund was raised in Hull to provide for her young son John's education. He went on to serve as an officer in the Second World War and was killed at Dunkirk.

A memorial plinth was erected at the KC Stadium, the new home of Hull FC, on VE Day, 11th December 2003 to honour Jack Harrison. Three years earlier the Army Rugby League had presented the Jack Harrison VC Memorial Trophy to the Combined Services Rugby League to be contested for annually in the Inter-Services fixture between the Army and the Royal Navy.

— ROSENFELD'S 80 TRY SEASON —

Nobody has ever scored more tries in a season that Albert Rosenfeld. The little Australian winger notched up 80 in the 1913/14 campaign while playing for Huddersfield, a total that proved beyond those other try-scoring greats Brian Bevan, Billy Boston and Martin Offiah.

Albert Aaron Rosenfeld was born in Sydney, the son of a Jewish tailor who played stand off for Eastern Suburbs. He was picked for the first Australian tour to England and Wales in 1908/09 but featured in only 15 of the 45 matches which included just one of the three Tests, and scored five tries.

However, one of those appearances included a 5–3 victory against Huddersfield who were impressed enough to sign him. The fact that he had fallen in love with a local mill manager's daughter obviously had an influence on his decision to stay in England.

'Rozzy', as he was known, was put on the wing and the move proved to be spectacularly successful as he became one of the greatest wingers in the British game. At just over 5ft 5ins, his low centre of gravity proved useful as his favourite tactic was to chip over the full back and sprint past him before re-gathering.

He got his Huddersfield career off to a flying start, scoring a couple of tries in his very first match against Broughton Rangers on 11th September 1909. He ended that first season with 24 and the following year notched up 40. In his third season he broke the Northern Union record with 78 tries but in the 1913/14 campaign he was to set a new benchmark.

Rosenfeld began the season by scoring four tries against York and ended up with a total of 80 from 42 appearances. They included seven tries in one game against amateurs Swinton Park in the Challenge Cup and he notched up five against both Leeds and Bramley. Incredibly he didn't score in his last three appearances of the season.

Rosenfeld's biggest ever haul in one game was the eight tries he ran in against Wakefield Trinity at Fartown on Boxing Day 1910. During his nine seasons with Huddersfield he scored a total of 388 tries.

His last game for the club was on 2nd April 1921, in a cup tie against Leeds. By then he had featured in 14 finals with Huddersfield, and won all but three of them. Rosenfeld went on to play for Wakefield and Bradford Northern before retiring in 1924. He died in Huddersfield in 1970 at the age of 85, the last survivor of that first Australian tour.

Brian Bevan of Warrington, came closest to his total when he scored 72 tries in 1952/53.

— SUCCESSIVE APPEARANCES —

Keith Elwell made a league record 242 consecutive appearances, including two as a substitute, for Widnes. The run started at Wembley in the 1977 Challenge Cup final against Leeds on 7th May.

The hooker began every match from then until his run of starting appearances ended at 239 after he played in a Lancashire Cup tie at home to St Helens on 5th September 1982. He was dropped for the match at Featherstone Rovers a week later, but went on as a substitute. He also played as a substitute in the next match and then started at Hull on 26th September 1982, before being left out of the squad for the next match.

— GOALS IN A CAREER —

Wigan staggered the rugby world in 1921 when they paid Jim Sullivan a then record-equalling £750 to leave Welsh rugby union. He was just 17. But the young full back proved to be worth every penny as he adorned rugby league for 25 years as one of its greatest ever players. He then went on to become a highly successful coach.

Sullivan still tops the list of the players who have scored the most goals in a career:

Goals	Scorer	Clubs	Career
2,867	Jim Sullivan	Wigan + (wartime) Dewsbury, Keighley, Bradford N.	1921–46
2,575	Neil Fox	Wakefield Tr., Bradford Northern, Hull Kingston Rovers, York, Bramley, Huddersfield	1956–79
1,768	Cyril Kellett	Hull Kingston R, Featherstone Rovers	1956–74
1,698	Kel Coslett	St Helens, Rochdale Hornets	1962–79
1,677	Gus Risman	Salford, Workington Town, Batley + (wartime) Dewsbury, Leeds, Bradford N., Hunslet	1929–54
1,591	John Woods	Leigh, Bradford Northern, Warrington, Rochdale H.	1976–92
1,578	Steve Quinn	York, Featherstone Rovers	1970–88
1,560	Jim Ledgard	Leeds, Dewsbury, Leigh	1944–61
1,478	Lewis Jones	Leeds	1952–64
1,460	Andrew Farrell	Wigan Warriors	1991–2004

— RUGBY LEAGUE LEGENDS: VINCE KARALIUS —

"Watch out, Karalius is coming!"

Vince Karalius was one of the toughest men ever to play rugby league. One of the few British players feared by the Australians, he was nicknamed 'The Wild Bull of the Pampas' on the 1958 tour to Australia and it is said that mothers would chide their errant children by warning them, "Karalius is coming".

Karalius was born on 15th October 1932 to a Scottish father and an Irish mother although his grandparents originated from Lithuania. His rugby league career began at a local amateur club, West Bank juniors, but he joined the professional ranks not with his hometown club but with St Helens, signing for them in August 1951.

Karalius was the perfect loose forward. Tough and uncompromising, he also had a shrewd rugby brain and was a clever ball player. He was one of the first players to realise the importance of fitness and is reputed to have run from his house in Widnes to training at St Helens and back, a round trip of some 20 miles.

An imposing figure with a rugged face and huge hands, his tackling technique involved taking opponents head on and wrapping his huge frame around them. He secured his reputation on the 1958 tour to Australia, manager Tom Mitchell insisting that the St Helens loose forward be included in the party, because he realised that they needed someone to take on the tough Aussie forwards.

Such was the impact of his ferocious tackling and rampaging runs that the Australian press, not noted for their willingness to shower praise on the opposition, gave him the 'Wild Bull' nickname that was to follow him throughout his career.

But he was much more than just a rough tough forward, showing his versatility by moving to stand off in the legendary second Test when skipper Alan Prescott played on with a broken arm.

In 1961 he led St Helens to Challenge Cup glory but a year later moved to his hometown club, Widnes. However this was never going to be a gentle winding down of his career.

"Some players come back to spend their last seasons at their own home town club like horses being put to grass," he said. "I came back to Widnes determined to give 100 per cent effort."

He was as good as his word, in his first season the club

finished third in the league and the following year he led them to their first trophy in 18 years with victory over Hull Kingston Rovers in the Challenge Cup final at Wembley.

Karalius retired in 1966 but in 1972 he came back to the club as coach and over the next three years Widnes won the Challenge Cup, the Lancashire Cup and were beaten finalists in the Regal Trophy and BBC2 Floodlit Trophy competitions. He coached Wigan from 1976 to 1979 and returned to Widnes for one final spell from May 1983 to May 1984. It's generally acknowledged that Karalius laid the foundations for the successful Widnes teams of the late 1970s and early 1980s. He was inducted into the RFL Hall of Fame in 2000.

Vincent Peter Patrick Karalius
Born: 15th October 1932 Widnes, Lancashire
Position: Loose forward
Playing career: 1952–66
Clubs: St Helens, Widnes,
International record: Great Britain (12 app)
Scoring: 51 tries

— EARLY BATHS —

Welshman Jim Mills is believed to hold the dubious honour of having been sent off more times than any other rugby league player. Mills had first use of the showers more than 20 times in his career with Halifax, Widnes, Workington Town, Wales and Great Britain.

While playing for Wales against New Zealand at Swansea in the 1975 World Cup, the prop forward trampled on prop John Greengrass and was banned for life by the New Zealand Rugby League. As a result, Mills had to withdraw from the 1977 World Cup which was held in New Zealand. His son David later played in Super League with the Widnes Vikings and Harlequins.

— SUPER LEAGUE RECORDS: PART THREE —

Longest try-scoring run: 11 matches by Richard Horne (Hull FC) 2006

Longest goal and point scoring run: 48 matches by Andrew Farrell (Wigan Warriors) 9th May 1997–22nd May 1999

Youngest player: Scott Moore (St Helens) was **16 years 213** days when he started at scrum half against the Wigan Warriors at the JJB Stadium on 20th August 2004 (born 23rd January 1988)

Oldest player: Brad Davis (Castleford Tigers) was **38 years 186 days** when he played as a substitute against the Wakefield Trinity Wildcats at Belle Vue on 16th September 2006 in the last match of the season (born 13th March 1968).

Highest team score: Bradford Bulls 96 Salford City Reds 16, 25th June 2000

Widest winning margin: 80 points, Leeds Rhinos 86 Huddersfield Giants 6, 16th July 1999 and Bradford Bulls 96 Salford City Reds 16, 25th June 2000

Highest away score: Warrington Wolves 12 Bradford Bulls 84, 9th September 2001

Widest away winning margin: 74 points, Leigh Centurions 0 Leeds Rhinos 74, 7th August 2005 and Leigh Centurions 4 St Helens 78, 4th September 2005

Lowest winning score and lowest points aggregate: Salford Reds 4 Castleford Tigers 0, 16th March 1997

Highest points aggregate: 112, Bradford Bulls 96 Salford City Reds 16, 25th June 2000

Most points by losing team: Leeds Rhinos 52 Huddersfield Giants **46,** 18th May 2001

Highest score draw: London Broncos 36 Leeds Rhinos 36, 18 July 2004

Longest winning run: 21, by Bradford Bulls, won last match of 1996 and first 20 of 1997 (also the longest unbeaten run)

Best opening run: 20 wins, by Bradford Bulls 1997

Longest losing run and run without a win: 27, by Halifax, 2003

Longest opening run without a win: 16, by Huddersfiel Giants, 2001. Lost first 15 and then drew

Biggest attendance: 25,004, Wigan Warriors v St Helens, 25th March 2005
Lowest attendance: 500, Paris St Germain v Salford Reds, 2nd July 1997
Lowest attendance at a British ground: 1,276, Halifax v London Broncos, 22nd August 2003
Biggest aggregate attendance for one round: 69,830 Round 7 (six matches), 24–25th March 2005
Record average for one round: 11,628 as above
Lowest aggregate attendance for one round: 24,099 Round 20 (six matches), 9–11th August 1996. Also lowest average for one round, 4,016

Note: These stats do not include play-off games.

— UP'N'UNDER —

Up'n'Under was a very successful stage play written by Yorkshireman John Godber who became artistic director of the Hull Truck Theatre Company in 1984. It was first performed there and won the Laurence Olivier Comedy of the Year Award in 1984. The play tells the story of an inept pub team in a rugby league sevens competition in Hull. Following a bet with the owner of the Cobblers Arms pub, they are given a bye to the final of the competition where they have to play the Cobblers.

The Cobblers Arms have been the best and most feared amateur rugby league team for the past 10 years. However, ex-pro Arthur bets their boss that he could train a bunch of deadbeats from the Wheatsheaf pub to defeat them in the tournament. But to do so he must first get them into shape, which he does with the help of fitness instructor Hazel Scott, who has her own gym.

It was made into a film in 1998 starring Samantha Janus, Gary Olsen, Neil Morrissey, Brian Glover, Griff Rhys Jones and Tony Slattery. The play was subsequently revived on stage with former England rugby union prop Gareth Chilcott in the Gary Olsen role.

— GREAT BRITAIN CAPTAINS —

Andrew Farrell captained Great Britain in every match from 1996 until his departure to rugby union in 2004 – a record 29 times. It brought the Wigan loose forward nine wins, two draws and 18 defeats.

A total of 66 players have captained Great Britain in Test, World Cup and Tri-Nations matches in 318 matches:

29 Andrew Farrell (Wigan) 1996–2004
19 Ellery Hanley (Bradford N, Wigan) 1987–91
17 Alan Prescott (St Helens) 1955–58
15 Eric Ashton (Wigan) 1958 -63
15 Jim Sullivan (Wigan) 1927–33
13 Garry Schofield (Leeds) 1991–94
11 Jonty Parkin (Wakefield T) 1921–30
10 Roger Millward (Hull KR) 1971–78
10 Harold Wagstaff (Huddersfield) 1914–22
 9 Frank Myler (St. Helens) 1970
 9 Gus Risman (Salford) 1936–46
 9 Clive Sullivan (Hull) 1972–73
 9 Ernest Ward (Bradford N) 1947–50
 8 Jamie Peacock (Bradford N, Leeds R) 2005–06
 8 Brian Noble (Bradford N) 1984
 8 Mike Gregory (Warrington) 1989–90
 7 James Lomas (Salford, Oldham) 1909–11
 6 Chris Hesketh (Salford) 1974
 6 Tommy Smales (Huddersfield, Bradford N) 1963–65
 5 Doug Laughton (Wigan, Widnes) 1970–79
 5 George Nicholls (St Helens) 1979
 5 Dickie Williams (Leeds, Hunslet) 1951–54
 4 Eric Fraser (Warrington) 1960–61
 4 Harry Pinner (St Helens) 1985–86
 4 Jeff Stevenson (York) 1959–60
 4 Dave Valentine (Huddersfield) 1954
 4 David Watkinson (Hull KR) 1986
 4 Shaun Edwards (Wigan) 1990–94
 3 Ernie Ashcroft (Wigan) 1954

3 Len Casey (Hull KR) 1980–1983
3 Brian Edgar (Workington T) 1966
3 Neil Fox (Wakefield T) 1966–68
3 Bill Holliday (Hull KR) 1967
3 Willie Horne (Barrow) 1952
3 Alex Murphy (St Helens) 1964–66
3 Bev Risman (Leeds) 1968
3 Harry Taylor (Hull) 1908
2 Tommy Bishop (St Helens) 1968–69
2 George Fairbairn (Wigan) 1980
2 Frank Gallagher (Batley) 1924
2 Jeff Grayshon (Bradford N) 1981–82
2 Alan Hardisty (Castleford) 1967
2 Phil Jackson (Barrow) 1958
2 Harry Poole (Leeds) 1966
2 Gwyn Thomas (Huddersfield) 1920
2 Derek Turner (Wakefield T) 1962
2 Johnny Whiteley (Hull) 1959–60
1 Arthur Atkinson (Castleford) 1936
1 Jim Brough (Leeds) 1936
1 Jack Cunliffe (Wigan) 1951
1 Joe Egan (Wigan) 1947
1 Les Fairclough (St Helens) 1929
1 Andy Goodway (Oldham) 1985
1 Syd Hynes (Leeds) 1971
1 Bert Jenkins (Wigan) 1908
1 Tommy McCue (Widnes) 1946
1 Keith Mumby (Bradford N) 1984
1 Steve Nash (Salford) 1982
1 Johnny Thomas (Wigan) 1911
1 David Topliss (Hull) 1982
1 David Ward (Leeds) 1981
1 Ted Ward (Wigan) 1947
1 Jonathan Davies (Widnes) 1992
1 Andy Platt (Wigan) 1993
1 Phil Clarke (Wigan) 1994
1 Paul Sculthorpe (St Helens) 2006

— RUGBY LEAGUE LEGENDS: REG GASNIER —

Reg Gasnier: The Dragon of St George

Nicknamed 'Puff the Magic Dragon' for his balanced running which saw him ghost past defenders, Reg Gasnier was one of the greatest Australian players of all time. A wonderfully skilful centre with great hands, pace and swerve, Gasnier in full flight was one of the great sights in rugby football.

A natural sportsman, Gasnier excelled at both rugby union

and cricket as a schoolboy but it was in rugby league with the Sydney club St George that he was to become a legend. He was 17 when he turned up at a St George pre-season training session and asked for a trial. He impressed enough to maintain a spot in the third grade side through 1958 and gained promotion to the first team the following season.

After just a handful of games Gasnier was selected to play for New South Wales, scoring three tries on debut. He was immediately picked for the Australian Test team for the three match series against the touring Kiwis. In the second Test he scored three tries and had a hand in another five as Australia hammered the New Zealanders. He was chosen to tour Great Britain and France with the 1959/60 Kangaroo tourists and in the opening match against Widnes showed his class by racing in for a 60-metre try with his first touch of the ball. Gasnier then underlined his class by collecting a hat-trick in Australia's 22–14 win over Great Britain at Swinton in the first Test although he was unable to prevent Great Britain winning the next two Tests and retaining the Ashes.

Three years later he became the youngest player ever to captain Australia when, at the age of 22, he led the Kangaroos in the home series against Great Britain. Eric Ashton's Lions were too strong for Australia, though, and took the series 2–1 but Gasnier led them in successful home series against South Africa and New Zealand in 1963.

Gasnier's second Kangaroo tour to Britain in 1963/64 confirmed his greatness. In a dream centre partnership with Graeme Langlands he scored two tries in their 28–2 victory over Great Britain in the first Test at Wembley and trounced them 50–12 at Swinton to take the Ashes.

On the club front Gasnier played a key role in St George's dominance of the Sydney premiership. In his first Grand Final for the Dragons in 1960 he scored two tries in their victory over Eastern Suburbs and appeared in St George's next five Premiership winning teams. He missed most of the 1966 season through injury but returned the following year and was in the side which lost the final to Canterbury in 1967 – which proved to be the final game of Gasnier's club career.

He returned to the Test team in that year leading Australia to success against the Kiwis and was appointed captain of his third and final Kangaroo tour. Australia retained the Ashes, but unfortunately Gasnier was cut down by a severe leg injury in the first Test against Great Britain. He did not reappear until the tour reached France.

In Avignon he took the field against a French provincial team but his leg gave way again and he had to be carried from the field on a stretcher. He never returned and his career was over at just 28.

The name Gasnier lives on in Australian rugby league. His nephew Mark, also a centre, followed him into the St George and Australia teams at the turn of the century.

Reg Gasnier
Born: May 12th 1939, Kogarah, New South Wales
Position: Centre
Playing career: 1959–67
Club: St George
International record: Australia (39 apps, 26 tries)
Scoring: 219 tries, 31 goals

— TRYING TIME? —

Matches without tries are a rarity in rugby league. Indeed it was only in the 12th season of Super League that a game was completed without a single touchdown.

On Friday 17th June 2007 bottom club Salford City Reds played Harlequins at The Willows. The match was played in a downpour and after a dour struggle Salford ran out 5–2 winners. The only scores came from the boot with Salford's John Wilshere kicking two penalties and Luke Robinson landing a drop goal. Quins' only points came from a Paul Sykes penalty.

— SEASIDE SHUFFLE —

The only team to rival Highfield's long and chequered history (see *Most Travelled*, page 56) is the club which began life in the Rugby Football League as Blackpool Borough in the 1954/55 season. However in 1987 they quit their ground at Borough Park and re-emerged as Springfield Borough, having relocated to Springfield Park, the original home of Wigan Athletic Football Club.

After one season they moved to Chorley and became Chorley Borough before moving on again the following season. This time they went to Altrincham to share with the local football club and became Trafford Borough.

A boardroom split saw a separate club formed at Chorley playing at Victory Park and they became Chorley Borough in the 1991–92 season. Trafford Borough, meanwhile, lasted three seasons before finding their way back to Blackpool playing the 1992/93 season as the Gladiators at the ground of Blackpool Mechanics FC but at the end of the season a re-constituted Second Division saw both Blackpool and Chorley in addition to Nottingham City, demoted to the National Conference.

Chorley regained their status in 1995/96 when they became Chorley Chieftains and played at Preston North End's Deepdale stadium. In 1997 they became Lancashire Lynx and were reasonably successful but at the end of the 1999/2000 season they were re-named Chorley Lynx. In 2004 Chorley Lynx folded.

But the story doesn't end there. A new team, the Blackpool West Coast Panthers, were created in 2005 although most of the personnel were former Chorley players. They initially played at Bloomfield Road but soon moved to ground share with Preston Grasshoppers rugby union club.

Now simply called the Blackpool Panthers, they briefly returned to Bloomfield Road. But after playing a few games at the ground of Fylde rugby union club, they signed a long-term deal to stay at their Woodlands Memorial Ground and currently have their administrative and commercial base there.

— LEAGUE V UNION —

Debate has raged for over a century about what would happen if a team of rugby league players played a team of rugby union players. In theory this could only happen after 1995 when union allowed professionalism but in fact matches featuring players from both codes had taken place over 50 years earlier.

The only environment where it could happen without reprisals from the union authorities was the armed forces. During the Second World War many league players were allowed to play international rugby union but, on 23rd January 1943, a match was staged between a rugby league side and a rugby union team.

It was played under union laws at Headingley and a crowd of 8,000 saw a Northern Command Rugby League XV beat a Northern Command Rugby Union XV 18–11. Another match was played on 24th April 1944 at Odsal between a Rugby League Combined Services side and a Rugby Union Combined Services, with the league side running out 15–10 winners. Bob Weighill, who later became a secretary of the RFU, played in the second game.

In 1996 the top sides in each code, Wigan and Bath, played in the first cross-code challenge. In the league encounter at Maine Road on 8th May Wigan won 82–6 while in the return game of union at Twickenham on 25th May, Bath defeated Wigan 44–19.

This was Wigan's second appearance at rugby union's HQ having earlier been invited to the Middlesex Sevens. On Saturday, 11th May 1996 they raced through to the final where they beat a Wasps side, captained by Lawrence Dallaglio, 38–15 in front of 61,000 fans.

Martin Offiah, who had been a beaten finalist with Rosslyn Park in 1987, claimed six of the 28 tries Wigan scored in the tournament. In 2002 the Bradford Bulls became the second rugby league team to win the prestigious Sevens.

— GROUND HOPPING —

Few clubs can claim to have used as many grounds for their home fixtures as the side that began as Fulham in 1980 and ended up as Harlequins in Super League. They kicked off at Craven Cottage, home to Fulham FC, but when they left there, the wandering began.

They have used three athletics stadiums in the capital, Crystal Palace, Barnet Copthall and Chiswick Polytechnic and played one-off games at non-league football grounds Wealdstone, Hendon, Crawley and Kingstonian (Kingsmeadow). They also played a game at Chelsea's Stamford Bridge before longer stints at Griffin Park, home of Brentford FC, and Charlton Athletic's The Valley.

In addition, the Londoners have played home matches at three Welsh rugby union grounds, Newport, Bridgend and Aberavon, and two English rugby union grounds, Welford Road, Leicester and the Stoop in Twickenham. The club have played 'home' fixtures at French grounds in Perpignan and Carcassone plus one at Tynecastle, home of Scottish football club Hearts.

This list does not include games at northern rugby league grounds which were classed as home fixtures.

— THE 2000 WORLD CUP —

The success of the 1995 competition should have set the template for future tournaments but the next World Cup, held in Britain and France in 2000, proved a disaster and plunged the Rugby Football League into a debt which took them four years to clear. The 12th tournament was perhaps too ambitious and it was dogged by atrocious weather.

Sixteen teams were divided into four pools but the decision to field a Lebanon team made up entirely of Australians of Lebanese descent, plus a Maori team alongside New Zealand opened the competition up to ridicule. At least the format was simple with the top two teams from each group progressing to the knock-out stages of quarter-finals, semi-finals then final.

There were some positives to come out of the tournament. The French performed well in front of some enthusiastic home crowds and the appearance of a Lebanon team led to the game being established in that middle eastern country.

New Zealand beat England to make the final while Australia were given a mighty fright by Wales in the other semi-final. A stunning first half performance by the Welsh saw them leading 22–14 early in the second half but the Kangaroos rallied and won through. Australia went on to beat the Kiwis 40–12 in the final with Brad Fittler lifting the newly restored original trophy.

The next World Cup is scheduled for Australia in 2008 to mark the centenary of Australian rugby league.

— SUNDAY BEST —

Rugby league was the first major sport in this country to adopt Sunday as its main fixture day. Declining gates in the mid-1960s led the move from Saturday, although by playing on Sunday the clubs faced the possibility of being prosecuted under the Sunday Observance Act of 1870 and came under fire from religious groups who wanted to keep the Sabbath special.

The first Sunday league fixtures took place on 17th December 1967 when Bradford Northern beat York 33–8 and Leigh overcame Dewsbury 15–10. In the early days clubs weren't allowed to charge on a Sunday so admission was by programme only.

More and more fixtures were played on Sunday and with healthy attendances ensuing, in 1977 the Rugby Football League declared Sunday to be their official match day. Leeds were one of the last clubs to switch from Saturday to Sunday. Clubs can now play on any day of the week with television often dictating not only the day but also the kick-off time.

— ATHLETES IN LEAGUE —

In the late 1950s and early 1960s a number of top class athletes decided to try their hand at rugby league, with varying degrees of success. The most high profile was Emmanuel McDonald Bailey from Trinidad and Tobago.

Bailey became a sprint sensation when he came over to Britain to join the RAF during the Second World War. He stayed on and in 1950 equalled the world record of 10.2 seconds for the 100 metres set by Jesse Owens in 1936. At the Helsinki Olympics in 1952 he became the first black athlete to win an Olympic medal for Britain with a bronze in the 100 metres. He retired from athletics in 1953 and in that year played a game of rugby league for Leigh.

The friendly against Wigan caused much media hype. It was played under the club's new floodlights and attracted a crowd of almost 15,000. However, after a less than distinguished performance, Bailey never played the game again.

Welsh sprinter Berwyn Jones fared far better. Jones had played a bit of union with his local club Rhymney, but it was in athletics that he made his mark. He won the bronze medal as a member of the British 4x100 metres relay team at the 1962 European Championships in Belgrade, Yugoslavia, alongside Alfred Meakin, Ronald Jones, and David Jones. He had been a British record-holder (10.3 seconds) and champion over 100 yards but in 1964 played a couple of trials for Wakefield Trinity. Jones signed for them and within nine months he was playing for Great Britain, scoring on his international debut against France in Perpignan.

Although selected for Great Britain's 1966 tour of Australia and New Zealand he did not make the Test team. In 1967/68, he was transferred to Bradford Northern, scoring 26 tries in his first season with them before moving to St Helens in 1969. He scored just two tries for the club before announcing his retirement. He died in January 2007 after a battle with motor neurone disease.

Alf Meakin, who had been in the sprint relay team with Jones in 1962, later played rugby league for Blackpool Borough while Oldham signed the European shot putt champion Arthur Rowe in 1962 but he never made the grade.

— GREAT COMEBACKS —

Any Batley Bulldogs fans who left when their side trailed 28–0 after only 26 minutes at Oldham on 21st August 2005 would have missed the most extraordinary comeback on record.

The Bulldogs had conceded five tries in less than half an hour of the National League One match. But Oldham did not score another try and Batley snatched a remarkable 34–32 victory with a converted try only five minutes from full time. Batley had pulled level at 28–28 after 51 minutes only for Oldham to edge back in front with two penalty goals. Then, just when it seemed their great fight back had been in vain, substitute John Gallagher completed a hat-trick on his debut and Darren Robinson added the match-winning goal.

The biggest deficit to be overcome in a Super League match was when Warrington Wolves won 22–21 at Wakefield Trinity Wildcats after trailing 21–0 on 26th March 2006. Warrington did not score their first points until the 47th minute and scored the match-winning converted try eight minutes form the end.

St Helens staged the best comeback in a Challenge Cup final when they recovered from being 26–12 down with 23 minutes remaining to beat Bradford Bulls 40–32 at Wembley in 1996.

The most impressive recovery in an Ashes Test came in 2003 when Great Britain led 20–8 just before half-time in the second Test at Hull. But a try just before the interval put Australia right back into the game and they snatched a 23–20 victory with a drop goal and penalty goal in the last five minutes.

— 1966 AND ALL THAT —

The 1966 Challenge Cup final between St Helens and Wigan at Wembley should have been a classic; instead it was instrumental in prompting two key changes in the way the game as played.

The 1961 final between these two giants of the game had produced a memorable contest and a capacity crowd of just over 98,000 came along five years later expecting another. However, events off the field were to conspire against this. The Wigan hooker, Colin Clarke, having been sent off before the final, was suspended and couldn't play so a utility forward, Tom Woosey, was drafted in.

Ironically, earlier in the season St Helens had signed the experienced hooker Bill Sayer from their arch rivals. Alex Murphy, the Saints skipper, knew they would have the upper hand in the scrums and sought to exploit this. In those days the penalty for going offside was merely a kick to touch followed by a scrum. Not surprisingly, St Helens were frequently caught offside with Sayer winning the ball from the ensuing scrum. With this glut of possession they had a stranglehold on the game and went on to win 21–2.

But it had been a deeply unsatisfying spectacle and the Rugby Football League vowed to do something about it. By the start of the next season the rules had been changed whereby after a kick to touch following a penalty, the game was re-started with a tap kick by the non-offending team, thus guaranteeing them possession.

In the BBC2 Floodlit Trophy of that season there was to be another innovation, the four tackle rule. This ensured that both teams would have an even chance of competing.

It was such a success that it was soon adopted for all competitions and in 1972 the number of tackles was increased to six.

— DUAL WELSH INTERNATIONALS —

More than 160 Welsh rugby union internationals, one in four from every team selected between 1881 and 1995, switched codes. Pontypool lost eight players in one season to rugby league.

Many former union players carved out very successful league careers with David Watkins, Jonathan Davies and David Young having the distinction of captaining Wales in both codes.

A total of 91 Welsh players have become dual internationals with a handful also representing the British Isles in both codes. Here is a list of the ten most-capped players who have played for Wales at league and union:

Name	Last RU club	First RL club	Move	Caps RU/RL
Scott Quinnell*	Llanelli	Wigan	1994	52 + 2
Scott Gibbs*	Swansea	St Helens	1994	53 + 3
David Young*	Cardiff	Leeds	1990	51 + 13
Allan Bateman*^#	Neath	Warrington	1990	35 + 12
Jonathan Davies^#	Llanelli	Widnes	1989	32 + 9
Steve Fenwick*	Bridgend	Cardiff Dragons	1981	30 + 2
Adrian Hadley	Cardiff	Salford	1988	27 + 9
Iestyn Harris^#	Cardiff Blues	Warrington	2001	25 + 15
Rob Ackerman*	Cardiff	Whitehaven	1986	22 + 5
David Watkins*^#	Newport	Salford	1967	21 + 16

* Rugby Union Test Lions
^ Rugby League Lions tourist
# GB rugby league cap

— TOP 10 SUPER LEAGUE CAREER DROP GOALS —

Goals	Player	Years
48	Lee Briers (Warrington, St Helens)	1997–2006
18	Graham Holroyd (Salford, Halifax, Leeds)	1996–2002
17	Paul Deacon (Bradford, Oldham)	1997–2006
15	Bobbie Goulding (Salford, Wakefield, Huddersfield, St Helens)	1996–2002
15	Brad Davis (Wakefield, Castleford)	1997–2006
15	Jamie Rooney (Wakefield, Castleford)	2003–06
14	Andrew Farrell (Wigan)	1996–2004
14	Willie Peters (Widnes, Wigan, Gateshead)	1999–04
11	Tommy Martyn (St Helens)	1996–2003
10	Sean Long (St Helens, Wigan)	1996–2006

Note: Stats correct up to and including season 2006.

— DEFUNCT COMPETITIONS —

Player's No6 Trophy

The increasing importance of sponsorship led to the introduction of this mid-season knock-out competition in the 1971/72 season. The cigarette company changed the name several times to fit in with whatever brand they wanted to promote. In 1977 it became the John Player Trophy and six years later was known as the John Player Special Trophy. In 1989, in its final incarnation, it was renamed the Regal Trophy. Televised on BBC's *Grandstand* programme on Saturday afternoons, the advent of Super League signalled the end of the competition with Wigan winning the last final against St Helens 25–16 at the McAlpine Stadium, Huddersfield on 13th January 1996. Blackpool Borough made their one and only appearance in a final in the 1976/77 competition, losing 25–15 to Castleford.

The Charity Shield
The shield was inaugurated in 1985 and copied the soccer template by pitting the champions against the cup holders in a pre-season match. However in 1990 and 1991, after Wigan had won both trophies, they played the Premiership winners. In 1992 and 1995, when Wigan captured all three trophies, they played the previous season's Division One runners-up. This was to be the last Charity Shield match. The man of the match in the Charity Shield was awarded the Jack Bentley Trophy, named after a well-known rugby league journalist.

The Captain Morgan Trophy
This was a competition for the first round winners in the Lancashire and Yorkshire Cups, which lasted just one season 1973–74. Warrington beat Featherstone Rovers 4–0 in the final played at Salford.

The Trans-Pennine Cup
This was a contest for the Second Division teams in 1998, based along county lines. The clubs finishing top of the table as a result of matches between teams of the same county played each other in the final. Batley topped the White Rose table and Oldham the Red Rose one, with Batley going on to win the final 28–12, their first trophy for 74 years.

The Treize-Tournoi
A cross-channel initiative played in 1998 featuring six teams: three from Britain, the First Division Grand Finalists and the Second Division champions, and the top three teams from the French Championship. Sponsored by media company EMAP, Lancashire Lynx surprisingly made the final and their players had to play for nothing because the club hadn't budgeted for it. They were beaten 16–10 by Villeneuve.

— TRANSFERS —

The Bosman ruling of 1997 had as much impact on rugby league as it did on football. The ruling stemmed from a court case won by Jean-Marc Bosman, a Belgian football player, which made players free agents once their contract with a club was up.

In 1999 the Rugby Football League declared that there would be no transfer fees for players over 24 years of age. This meant an end to the big transfers because clubs would usually wait until a player was out of contract before offering him a deal.

Given the change in circumstances it seemed that the £440,000 Wigan paid Widnes for Martin Offiah in January 1992 would be a record that would never be beaten. However, in the early part of the 2006 season Wigan found themselves bottom of the Super League and in danger of being relegated. They sacked their coach Ian Millward and replaced him with Brian Noble of the Bradford Bulls.

In order to bolster their pack, they also struck a deal with the Bulls for their Great Britain prop Stuart Fielden, who was still under contract. The Warriors paid £450,000 to bring Fielden to the JJB Stadium in June, which broke the record amount they had paid for Offiah 15 years previously. Wigan avoided relegation but were subsequently docked four points for breaches of the salary cap.

The deal which took Paul Newlove from the Bradford Bulls to St Helens in November 1995 was believed to be the biggest ever, worth £500,000. However it was made up of £250,000 in cash plus centre Paul Loughlin and forwards Bernard Dwyer and Sonny Nickle.

Offiah was involved in a unique transfer a year later when he left Wigan. In a deal thought to total £300,000. Offiah signed a joint deal to play rugby union for Bedford and rugby league for the London Broncos although he gave up the union part of the deal after a year.

— GROUNDS FOR CHANGE —

Towards the end of the 20th century many of the grounds that had been synonymous with the first 100 years of rugby league began to disappear. The tragic fire at Valley Parade, home to Bradford City FC, in 1985 and the Hillsborough disaster four years later led to the Taylor Report which imposed stringent new safety regulations on sports grounds.

This hit rugby league hard with many clubs simply unable to update their facilities and subsequently forced to vacate historic homes, often with dire consequences. With St Helens, Salford, Wakefield, Castleford and Leigh all planning to move to new sites, few original stadiums will remain and those that do will have changed almost beyond recognition. At the top level only Bradford and Leeds intend to stay at their original grounds, although both these stadiums have been or are scheduled to be revamped.

In a number of cases, the sale of a ground has not been followed by a move to a new purpose-built stadium so many clubs were forced into sharing or, even worse, destined to wander from ground to ground like some latter-day Flying Dutchman, never to settle.

Many grounds rich in rugby league heritage have been lost forever and the clubs, which were rooted in the community, have never really recovered.

- Station Road, the home of Swinton for many years, was one of the most important grounds in rugby league. It hosted Challenge Cup semi-finals, Lancashire cup finals, and Top 16 play-off finals in addition to many internationals.

  The Lions were one of the powers in the game in the early 1960s and their ground was one of the best when it opened in 1929. It was still a regular venue for finals and internationals in the 1960s but the decline of the team in the 1970s heralded the end of the line for Station Road.

In season 1991/92 the Lions could only muster three league wins and their defeat to local rivals Salford on 20th April 1992 was to be their last at the ground. Within weeks came news that the ground had been sold to become a housing development. The club subsequently moved in with Bury football club and later played at Salford City football club's ground at Kersal before agreeing to a ground-share with rugby union club Sedgley Park.

- Oldham's is a similar tale, although to all but diehard fans their Watersheddings ground was an inhospitable place. Situated at the foot of the Pennines, it was the home of the rugby league team from 1889 until 1997. Ironically, for one of the coldest grounds you could ever wish to play rugby on, its demise coincided with the advent of summer rugby. Even the final game at Watersheddings, scheduled for December 1996, had to be postponed because the pitch was frost bound.

  The renamed Oldham Bears were original members of Super League and played at Boundary Park, home of Oldham Athletic football club, but when the Bears were relegated they soon found themselves homeless and have struggled to find a permanent home ever since.

- Blackpool Borough had the newest ground in the rugby league when they opened Borough Park in 1963. However, following the Bradford fire it would have cost the struggling Blackpool team too much to comply with new ground regulations. The final first team match at Borough Park was played in January 1987 after which the club led a nomadic existence and underwent several name changes over the years. A new club calling themselves the Blackpool Panthers emerged in 2005, playing at Blackpool FC's Bloomfield Road ground, but that arrangement didn't last long and they subsequently went to share with Fylde rugby union club.

- Halifax quit their old Thrum Hall home in 1998 to share with Halifax Town football club at their newly revamped ground the Shay. However, lack of finances meant that the East Stand couldn't be completed and what could be a fine facility remains blighted by the unfinished building work.
- Rochdale Hornets quit their original home, the Athletic Grounds, in 1988 and moved in with their soccer neighbours Rochdale AFC. This has been one of the few successful ground-share stories with the facilities at Spotland considered to be the best outside Super League.

— LEAGUE'S HERITAGE —

Rugby league hasn't been too good at preserving its past, and it took former Great Britain international turned Sky commentator Mike Stephenson to finally create a legacy for future generations.

Stevo has been a collector of memorabilia all his life and thanks to his efforts an exhibition featuring many of his mementos has been set up at the George Hotel in Huddersfield where the sport was born in 1895.

In 2005 the hotel became home to a permanent exhibition celebrating the game's history. Called the Gillette Rugby League Heritage Centre, it has a collection of rare memorabilia, ancient caps and jerseys, valuable medals and trophies, old programmes and pictures.

The centre uses plasma screens and floor-to-ceiling graphics to chart the game's progress and includes a collection of over 200 framed prints in the hotel's public areas. The main displays are in a purpose built exhibition hall and are well worth a visit.

— RUGBY LEAGUE LEGENDS: JEAN GALIA —

The magnifique Jean Galia

Jean Galia was single-handedly responsible for introducing rugby league to France. A rugby union international and former boxer, he saw his international career stopped in its tracks when the French were expelled from the International Championship over allegations of professionalism. Then his club Villeneuve were suspended by the French governing body for poaching players so the resourceful Galia began to look elsewhere,

An Australian entrepreneur called Harry Sunderland staged an exhibition match of rugby league between an Australian and an English team at the Pershing Stadium in Paris in December 1933. Galia and some of his rugby union playing colleagues went to the game and he was so impressed that he decided to take up the sport. Within three months he had put a French side together which came to England to play matches at Wigan, Leeds and London.

He returned enthused, determined to set up a French rugby league competition and in August 1934 12 clubs kicked off the new venture. Not surprisingly, Galia's Villeneuve club were the first champions.

Five years later he led France to their first International Championship and French rugby league or 'Rugby À Treize' as it became known, was off and running. However, the outbreak of war was to change everything (see *Rugby À Treize*, page 80). Under the wartime Vichy government the game was banned and the clubs had their funds seized. The game in France was dealt a body blow, which it has struggled to recover from.

Despite being almost 29 when he took up rugby league, Galia was a natural at the game, being a tough, uncompromising forward as well as an impressive leader. Off the field his vision and drive would have undoubtedly have helped the sport recover after the war but he died in 1949 aged just 43.

Jean Galia
Born: 20th May 1905, Ille-sur-Tet, France
Position: Second row forward
Club: Villeneuve
International record: France (5 apps)

— BRANDING RIGHTS —

The trend for selling the naming rights to grounds has infiltrated rugby league. Although some supporters are opposed to the idea, it's understandable when teams move to new homes that they want to generate extra revenue by branding the ground with a sponsor's name. So we've had the Huddersfield Giants playing at the McAlpine (later Galpharm) Stadium, Wigan operating from the JJB Stadium, Hull at the KC Stadium and Warrington at the Halliwell Jones.

However, slapping a new name on an old ground rarely works. Wakefield's Belle Vue home became the Atlantic Solutions Stadium for a while and Odsal was re-branded the Grattan Stadium.

Neither of those name changes caught the imagination of fans, but it was a different story at Castleford. The club's Wheldon Road ground reeks of rugby league history but when Castleford added Tigers to their name for Super League an internet company called jungle.com decided to sponsor them and the venue became known as the Jungle.

Although the sponsorship has come to an end, the club decided to continue to call their home the Jungle, although no doubt when they get their new stadium the Jungle name won't be going with them.

One of the more bizarre ground naming sagas concerned Leigh's Hilton Park. With the coming of summer rugby they decided, like most other clubs, to give themselves a nickname. As it was 1995 and Leigh had been one of the original founders of the Northern Union in 1895 they decided on a tie-in with their centenary celebrations and opted for Centurians. However, when artwork was prepared for the new logo it featured a Roman centurion, complete with plumed helmet! Leigh quickly decided to change the spelling of their nickname to Centurions and their then coach, Paul Terzis, completed the Roman theme by suggesting they re-name the ground the Coliseum. This they did but everyone still called it Hilton Park and eventually the Coliseum was consigned to history.

But spare a thought for the club who started it all. Keighley were years ahead of their time when a couple of enterprising directors, Mike Smith and Mick O'Neill, brought the razzmatazz of American sports to the Yorkshire club in the early 1990s.

They added the nickname Cougars, changed Lawkholme Lane into Cougar Park and transformed the match-day experience with music and dancing girls. The club involved the community, especially kids, and Cougarmania took off. Keighley began to attract good crowds and when they won the old Second Division title in 1995 it looked like they were destined for the new top tier competition called Super League. However, the Rugby Football League denied them a place in the new elite. There was a suggestion that their facilities weren't up to scratch but basically they powers-that-be didn't see them as a Super League team unlike the London Broncos who finished fourth in the Second Division in 1994/95 when Keighley were champions.

Snubbed by the Super League, the Keighley dream died. Many in rugby league had frowned on their brash marketing ideas but within a few years, virtually every club in the league had adopted the Cougars' approach.

— QUICKEST SENDING OFF —

Adrian Morley raced into the record books when the Great Britain forward flattened Australia's Robbie Kearns only seven seconds into the first Test of the 2003 Ashes series.

Morley charged 40 metres from the kick-off to catch Kearns with a forearm smash to the chin. The incident stunned the crowd who were in the JJB Stadium, Wigan, although many latecomers would have missed seeing the blow. Referee Steve Ganson took his time, consulting with touch judge Steve Wright and video referee David Campbell, before showing the Sydney Roosters prop the red card. The depleted British side put up a great show before losing 22–18.

There is no record of a quicker dismissal and it is certainly the fastest in any Test match. Despite the offence, Morley was cleared to play in the next two Tests, which Britain also lost narrowly. In 2007 Morley, playing in Super League with the Warrington Wolves and with his bad boy days behind him, was made captain of the Great Britain side who took on France at Headingley on 22nd June 2007.

— CLUBS SINCE 1895 —

Club	First season	Last season	Name changes
Aberdare	1908/09	1908/09	-
Acton & Willesden	1935/36	1935/36	-
Altrincham	1901/02	1901/02	-
Barrow	1900/01	-	Barrow Braves Barrow Border Raiders Barrow Raiders
Barry	1908/09	1908/09	-
Batley	1895/96	-	Batley Bulldogs
Birkenhead Wanderers	1901/02	1904/05	-
Blackpool Borough^	1954/55	1992/93	Springfield Borough Chorley Borough Trafford Borough Blackpool Gladiators
Blackpool Panthers	2005	-	-
Bradford	1895/96	-	Bradford Northern Bradford Bulls
Bramley	1896/97	1999	-
Brighouse Rangers	1895/96	1905/06	-
Broughton Rangers	1895/96	1954/55	Belle Vue Rangers
Cardiff	1951/52	1951/52	-
Cardiff City	1981/82	1984/85	Bridgend
Carlisle	1981/82	1997	Carlisle Border Raiders
Carlisle City	1928/29	1928/29	-
Castleford (1)	1896/97	1905/06	-

Club	First season	Last season	Name changes
Castleford (2)	1926/27	-	Castleford Tigers
Catalans Dragons	2006	-	-
Celtic Crusaders	2006	-	-
Chorley	1989/90	2004	Chorley Borough Chorley Chieftains Chorley Lancashire Lynx Chorley Lynx
Coventry	1910/11	1912/13	-
Dewsbury	1901/02	-	Dewsbury Rams
Doncaster	1951/52	-	Doncaster Dragons Doncaster Lakers
Ebbw Vale	1907/08	1911/12	-
Featherstone Rovers	1921/22	-	-
Fulham	1980/81	-	London Crusaders London Broncos Harlequins RL
Gateshead Thunder (1)	1999	1999	-
Gateshead Thunder (2)	2000/01	-	-
Goole	1901/02	1901/02	-
Halifax	1895/96	-	Halifax Blue Sox Halifax
Heckmondwike	1896/97	1898/99	-
Holbeck	1896/97	1903/04	-

Club	First season	Last season	Name changes
Huddersfield	1895/96	-	Huddersfield Barracudas Huddersfield Giants (Huddersfield and Sheffield Giants)
Hull	1895/96	-	Hull Sharks, Hull FC
Hull Kingston Rovers	1899/00	-	-
Hunslet	1895/96		New Hunslet, Hunslet, Hunslet Hawks
Keighley	1901/02	-	Keighley Cougars
Kent Invicta	1983/84	1984/85	Southend Invicta
Lancaster	1901/02	1904/05	-
Leeds	1895/96	-	Leeds Rhinos
Leeds Parish Church	1896/97	1900/01	-
Leigh	1895/96	-	Leigh Centurions
Liverpool City	1906/07	1906/07	-
Liversedge	1895/96	1901/02	-
London Skolars	2003	-	-
Manningham	1895/96	1902/03	-
Mansfield Marksman^	1984/85	1992/93	Nottingham City
Merthyr Tydfil	1907/08	1910/11	-
Mid/Rhondda	1908/09	1908/09	-
Millom	1899/00	1905/06	-
Morecambe	1896/97	1898/99	-
Newcastle	1936/37	1937/38	-
Normanton	1901/02	1905/06	-

Club	First season	Last season	Name changes
Oldham	1895/96	-	Oldham Bears Oldham
Paris St. Germain	1996	1997	-
Pontefract	1903/04	1906/07	-
Pontypridd	1926/27	1927/28	-
Radcliffe	1901/02	1901/02	-
Rochdale Hornets	1895/96	-	-
Runcorn	1895/96	1914/15	-
Salford	1896/97	-	Salford Reds Salford City Reds
Scarborough Pirates	1991/92	1991/92	-
Sheffield Eagles	1984/85	-	-
South Shields	1902/03	1903/04	-
South Wales	1996	1996	-
Sowerby Bridge	1901/02	1901/02	-
St Helens	1895/96	-	-
St Helens Recreation	1919	1938/39	-
Stockport	1895/96	1902/03	-
Streatham & Mitcham	1935/36	1936/37	-
Swinton	1896/97	-	Swinton Lions
Treherbert	1908/09	1909/10	-
Tyldesley	1895/96	1899/00	-
Wakefield Trinity	1895/96	-	Wakefield Tr. Wildcats
Warrington	1895/96	-	Warrington Wolves
Whitehaven	1948/49	-	Whitehaven Warriors Whitehaven
Widnes	1895/96	-	Widnes Vikings
Wigan	1895/96	-	Wigan Warriors

Club	First season	Last season	Name changes
Wigan Highfield	1922/23	1997	London Highfield Liverpool Stanley Liverpool City Huyton Runcorn Highfield Highfield Prescot Panthers
Workington Town	1945/46	-	-
York	1901/02	-	Ryedale/York York York Wasps

* Old Castleford club
^ Demoted to Nat. Conf. League for 1993/94 and never regained senior status

Selected Bibliography

Tony Collins, *Rugby's Great Split, Class, Culture and the Origins of Rugby League Football* (Frank Cass, 1998)

Ray French's 100 Greatest Rugby League Players (Queen Anne Press, 1989)

Robert Gate, *Rugby League Fact Book* (Guinness Publishing, 1991)

Robert Gate, *Rugby League An Illustrated History* (Arthur Barker, 1989)

Les Hoole, *The Rugby League Challenge Cup, An Illustrated History* (Breedon Books, 1998)

John Huxley, *Rugby League Challenge Cup* (Guinness Publishing, 1992)

Mike Latham, *British Rugby League, A Groundhopper's Guide* (League Publications Ltd, 2005)

Garry Schofield with Neil Hanson, *Garry Schofield's Rugby League Masterpieces* (Sidgwick & Jackson, 1995)

The Rugby League World Cup, An illustrated history of Rugby's oldest global tournament (League Publications Ltd, 2000)